THE MILFORD S
Popular Writers o
Volume Twenty-Fi

Science Fiction Voices #2
Interviews with science fiction writers conducted by **Jeffrey M. Elliot**

Featuring...
RAY BRADBURY
LARRY NIVEN
A. E. van VOGT
POUL ANDERSON
ROBERT SILVERBERG

With a new introduction by Richard A. Lupoff

R. REGINALD

THE *Borgo Press*

SAN BERNARDINO, CALIFORNIA

MCMLXXIX

To Gene, Harriet, and Janine—
With Love and Appreciation

CONTENTS

Introduction, by Richard A. Lupoff	3
Foreword	8
Larry Niven: Science Fiction's Master World-Builder	9
Ray Bradbury: Poet of Fantastic Fiction	20
A. E. van Vogt: A Writer with a Winning Formula	30
Poul Anderson: Seer of Far-Distant Futures	41
Robert Silverberg: Next Stop—*Lord Valentine's Castle*	51

Abbreviations Code: JE=Jeffrey Elliot; LN=Larry Niven; VV=A. E. van Vogt; PA=Poul Anderson; RB=Ray Bradbury; RS=Robert Silverberg

National Serials Data Program Cataloging:

Science fiction voices. 1-

    (The Milford Series: Popular writers of today ; v. 25)
No subject headings or classification numbers have yet been assigned.

sn79-1396

ISBN 0-89370-137-8 (Cloth edition; $8.95)
ISBN 0-89370-237-4 (Paper edition; $2.95)

OCLC#4579150

Copyright © 1979 by Jeffrey Elliot.
Portions of the interviews in this book have appeared first in the following publications: "An Interview with Larry Niven" in *Questar*, copyright © 1979 by Questar Magazine; "Interview with Ray Bradbury" in *The San Francisco Review of Books*, Copyright © 1977 by The San Francisco Review of Books; "A Conversation with Ray Bradbury" in *The Diversifier*, Copyright © 1978 by The Diversifier; "Interview: Ray Bradbury" in *Future Magazine*, Copyright © 1978 by Future Magazine, Inc.; "Interview: Poul Anderson" in *Galileo*, Copyright © 1979 by Galileo Magazine; "Interview: Robert Silverberg" in *Future Magazine*, Copyright © 1979 by Future Magazine, Inc. All rights reserved. No part of this book may be reproduced in any form without the expressed written consent of the publisher. Published by arrangement with the author. Printed in the United States of America by Griffin Printing & Lithograph Co., Glendale, CA.

Produced, designed, and published by R. Reginald, The Borgo Press, P. O. Box 2845, San Bernardino, CA 92406, USA. Composition by Mary Burgess. Cover design by Judy Cloyd Graphic Design. Cloth binding by California Zip Bindery, San Bernardino, CA.

First Edition———October, 1979

INTRODUCTION

You're about to read a book of interviews with science fiction authors. An obvious question is, *Why?* Why bother to read an interview with an author? If you're interested in a given person's works, all you have to do is pick them up and read them. If you want critical explications, pick up some good book *about* science fiction. There didn't used to be any of those but there are plenty of 'em now.

But why pester the authors themselves with questions, and scribble down their replies, and put them together in books like *Science Fiction Voices?* I suppose, for starters, there's a certain prurient interest in the authors because they are, will they or nil they, public figures of a sort, through their works if not *in propriae personae*. Like movie stars, authors discover that people want to know all about them—how their homes are furnished, what they eat for breakfast, which small town in the Midwest they grew up in, their personal preferences in music, bed-partners, alcoholic beverages and automobiles.

As the author of a number of science fiction novels, I have myself been asked to submit to a few interviews, to appear as a guest at some fan conventions, and so on. And I have been told more than once that I have become a "star." I must say that I find this *very* difficult to live with. Of course, one wants to write the best book one can (being no different from a seller of used cars or a pastry chef, who wants to do the best possible job of selling used cars or baking pastries). But why must one's *self*, one's most personal biographical and emotional sensitivities, be placed under a floodlight?

One of the worst moments I have ever experienced occurred in a city several hundred miles from my home. I had spent the afternoon at a bookstore there signing books for fans, chatting with strangers, being just as charming and modest as I could be. In a way, it was pleasant work—certainly bolstering to the ego. And yet it was harrowing—I felt as if I were being bitten off and devoured emotionally by people whom I didn't know, who didn't know me, but who had paid their dollar-ninety-five for my latest paperback and were consequently the owners in fee simple not merely of a dollar-ninety-five's worth of book but a dollar-ninety-five's worth of *me*!

The ordeal over, I escaped to my motel for a shower and a change of clothes, and my wife and I headed for a favorite restaurant for dinner. The place was dark, comfortable; the food was good; and we were anonymous. We finished our meal, went through the usual ceremony of exchanging credit card for tabulation, got back the card, put down a tip and headed for the exit.

Just as I reached for the door-handle, the waitress raced to my side, placed her hand on my sleeve, and demanded, "Wait! I need your autograph before you go!"

My wife told me later that even in the dim restaurant she could see, at that moment, my face turn white as death. I know that I felt the blood rush from my face and my hands grow cold and begin to tremble.

"Here, sir," the waitress said, "you forgot to sign the slip. American Express won't accept the charge without your signature."

Reprieved—reprieved at the very foot of the gallows!

And that was the result of "stardom." No one has, thank heaven, ever called me a "superstar." At least, not yet. I suspect that if anyone ever does, I shall have to fight down simultaneous and conflicting impulses to commit murder and/or suicide.

But, of course, we *are* creatures of conflicting impulses. At the same time that we dodge the spotlight, we also pursue it. Most authors crave attention—but, O! if only we could cause that attention to be directed to our works rather than to our persons!

* * * * *

There are, of course, better reasons than mere prurience to be interested in the creators of works we admire. For one, we will probably understand and appreciate those works more fully if we understand the context in which they are created. To know the times, the locale, the circumstances under which were written *Cymbeline, The Charterhouse of Parma, The Tale of the Genji*, is better to understand those works. To know and understand their respective authors is to receive an incalculable aid in this purpose.

And there is the admiration of heroes. We do wish to identify ourselves, to associate with, in some manner to blend our lives with, those we admire. In this little field of science fiction, I never met or corresponded with Mary Shelley, H. G. Wells, H. P. Lovecraft or Edgar Rice Burroughs. But I did meet—at least to shake hands with—"Doc" Smith, Hugo Gernsback, Edmond Hamilton, Leigh Brackett, Miriam Allen deFord, Hannes Bok, Otto Binder, Anthony Boucher, Ed Earl Repp. Gone now, all of them. And of those still living, Jack Williamson, Frank Belknap Long, Stanton A. Coblentz, C. L. Moore, Fritz Leiber, and uncounted others less senior in the rolls.

The interviews published in this book give us all a chance to know the authors involved.

It would seem, on the face of it, that interviewing should be the easiest form of journalism. Especially in this day of miniaturized cassette-loaded tape recorders, all you have to do is go to somebody's house and chat for an hour. Then transcribe your tape, clean out the *umms* and the surplus *Well, I supposes*, and you're in business.

Not so!

Some interviewees are helpfully forthcoming, will volunteer relevant data, and speak in a pleasantly discursive and anecdotal fashion. But others . . . .

A while ago I heard a prominent actor being interviewed over the radio. The show was done "live," so there was no opportunity to edit tape. The actor was most expressive and forthcoming when armed with a script—I'd seen his films and he was certainly articulate in them. But before a live microphone and without a script to work from, he lapsed into silence. The interviewer—to whom my heart went out—struggled desperately to ask leading questions, mention provocative names, elicit substantial answers.

Nothing.

In response to a direct question, the famous actor would go as far as "Yes," or "No," or—most often—"I don't remember." And that was all he would say!

(He was, at the time, supposedly promoting his autobiography. I'm sure it was ghost-written, and it would have been wiser to send out a ghost on the promotional tour, too!)

At the other extreme, there's someone like Alfred Bester. In one interview which I recently read, Alfie simply took over both roles. He totally ignored the interviewer, supplied his own questions, provided his own answers, and made a marvelously entertaining—but utterly unrevealing—show of it.

And yet my all-time favorite interview—again, this one took place on "live" radio—was with Ayn Rand. The interviewer, who specialized in the provocative thrust to get his subjects riled up, opened the interview with the following words. (I don't have them on tape, unfortunately, but they are engraved on the plates of my memory.)

"Welcome, Miss Ayn Rand, author and creator of the philosophy of Objectivism. Objectivism, Miss Rand's philosophy of life, is based on the proposition that I've got mine, and everybody else can just go to hell."

"Where did you get that idea?" Rand asked.

"Well, it's so, isn't it?" the interviewer asked back.

"Did you find that in one of my works?"

"Well, it's there, isn't it?"

"Have you read any of my works? *The Fountainhead*? *Atlas Shrugged*?"

"I'm afraid I haven't, but—"

"Have you read *anything* of mine?"

"No, but I'm told—"

"Never mind what you've been told. If you wish to interview me you must first read my works. Or at least one of them—any one of them. You haven't done that, so you aren't qualified to interview me. Good day."

And she left! She just got up and walked out of the studio, leaving the poor fish of a broadcaster floundering as if he'd been pulled out of the water and left to drown in the air!

*   *   *   *   *

There have been a lot of interviews with science fiction authors published lately. Some of them are very good, some very bad. I've seen two earlier books of them, one by Darrell Schweitzer and one by Paul Walker, and while both have their definite value, I am inclined to think that *Science Fiction Voices #2* is the best one yet.

Jeffrey Elliot is a man who does his homework. That last word has a number of relevancies, the most literal one being academic. Elliot holds a doctorate in Government and his major occupation is teaching. He is also a prolific author in areas both in and out of his academic field. His most recent book is *Keys to Economic Understanding*. His journalistic efforts have included interviews with scores of figures ranging from members of Congress and labor leaders to poets to mayors to political activists to general ("mainstream") novelists.

I think we're lucky to have him working in the area of science fiction. He says, "Science fiction fills me with excitement, delight, and optimism. It challenges my imagination and rekindles my spirit." And he likes science fiction *writers*. "As a group, they're extraordinarily interesting and stimulating . . . highly articulate, literate, and talented."

When he prepares to interview an author, he invests heavily in preparation: an investment of time and energy. He scours the bookshops and libraries to find everything he can by the author. He reads not only that author's works, but everything he can find that has been written *about* the author.

He goes to the trouble of tracking people who know the author and who are willing to share with him their own perspectives on the author and his or her work.

Before he ever makes his call on the subject, he thinks through the direction, the *shape*, of the interview—and prepares anywhere from 50 to 100 questions. And then he tapes anywhere from several hours to several days of conversations with the subject.

Jeff had me on that griddle awhile ago. He arrived at my home shortly after breakfast, armed with a tape recorder, a pad of ammunition, and a pocket full of tapes. We worked all through the morning—and it was work, although by no means unpleasant. We "broke" for lunch in the company of Jeff's photographer, but although the tape recorder was left behind, the inquisition did not cease. And after dessert and coffee, it was back to the house and back to work, until very nearly dinner time.

Then Jeff departed, and when I next heard from him, he had transcribed and edited his tapes, and sent me the interview for the checking of spellings and the like.

Clearly, he expended huge effort and took pains to do his job. And the result showed the effort to be well spent. Why—in the transcript I come across as intelligent, thoughtful, and sensitive. Talk about making a silk purse! (You won't find that interview in this book, by the way—but if you hunt around you should be able to find its magazine incarnation. And there will be more volumes in this Borgo Press series.)

Of the scores of interviews Jeff Elliot has conducted, I think the five he selected for this book represent an excellent spectrum of writers, by personality and by works. We have the scientific intellect whose works, for better or for worse, are virtually all idea. We have the poet of space, whose tales are all emotion and image. We meet the unorthodox psychologist whose latest project—as revealed in Elliot's interview with him—is the simultaneous mastery of some 200 languages! We have a man who could be called a carpenter of words, whose works of fiction are as carefully planned and as precisely executed as a perfect lintel or joist. And we have the artist reborn, a onetime self-defined hack who grew into science fiction's single finest novelist—and then quit cold—and is now at work again, on his first novel since 1974!

I have no quarrel—not one syllable—with Elliot's inclusion of these five authors. I *do* wish that there were other representation that is *not* present in this book. All of the authors here are veterans. One of them mentions, in his section, that he has been selling fiction for 17 years. And he's the *newest* of the writers represented! I'd like to see somebody younger in Jeffrey Elliot's next batch of interviews. I'd also like to see some women—the present five authors are all men—and someone non-white—and someone from a country and a culture other than that of the United States.

But all of that will come in later volumes, I am sure.

The present, you will find informative, entertaining, enlightening. It's as gripping as good fiction itself. In fact, Jeff Elliot sent me a copy of his manuscript for reading and inadvertently left out one page. I was reading the book, virtually mesmerized, when the discontinuity in the text leaped out and hit me like a bucket of ice-water! It was all inadvertent, of course. But what a tribute to the quality of the work, that a one-page break could produce such a shock!

It *was* inadvertent, of course.

I think.

Richard A. Lupoff
January, 1979

FOREWORD

This volume comprises five in-depth interviews with several leading writers in the science fiction field—Larry Niven, Ray Bradbury, A. E. van Vogt, Poul Anderson, and Robert Silverberg. The interviews are intended to provide the reader with a glimpse of each writer as pictured through his own words. In the course of reading each interview, it is hoped that the reader will come away with a better understanding of the writer and his attitudes toward his craft.

The interviews are not intended as the final word on the writers represented here, nor are they presented as the definitive statement on their opinions and beliefs. Instead, the aim of this volume is to foster a deeper appreciation of each writer—who he is, why he writes, what he thinks, how he works, what he hopes to accomplish, and how he views his craft.

The interviews were conducted at each author's home or office, extending over a period of several hours and, in some cases, days. Minor editing has been done to facilitate communication, but a conscious attempt has been made to leave each interview intact as much as possible, believing that this approach will better capture the style, content, and spirit of the writer.

This interviewer has endeavored to pose a wide range of questions, touching on various subjects of interest and concern. Obviously, other questions could have been asked or those that were asked could have been phrased in a different manner. No effort has been made to whitewash or condemn. Instead, this interviewer has sought to present the testimony of five outstanding practitioners in the field, hoping that such testimony will contribute to a keener awareness of how these writers go about the business of inventing science fiction and setting it down on paper. The interviews represent no special order, and may be read in a variety of ways.

LARRY NIVEN:

Science Fiction's Master World-Builder

As I drove to Tarzana, California, the home of science fiction superstar, Larry Niven, I wondered about this galactic talent and his universe, the birthplace of the "Thrints," "Bandersnatchi," "Puppeteers," and so many other engaging characters. When I arrived at his home, I was greeted at the door by the author himself, who ushered me into his living room. Niven promptly excused himself, retreating into the kitchen, where he hurriedly concocted us a brandy and coffee. During his absence, I gazed around the room. It, like the rest of the house, is large, airy, and inviting. The walls are tastefully adorned with science fiction art, giving the house a sort of space-age look. The mood is further enhanced by several large wall posters, which are color enlargements of various Niven book jackets, as well as several Dali lithographs, all of which tastefully complement the futuristic flavor of the house. Indeed, it is here that the author penned such memorable stories as *World Out of Time*, *Tales of Known Space*, *The Long Arm of Gil Hamilton*, *Inferno* (with Jerry Pournelle), *The Magic Goes Away*, and *Convergent Series*.

In addition to the numerous works of art which embellish the walls, Niven's home is stacked high with books—all sizes, shapes, and kinds. It is clear, though, that the author has a special fondness for science fiction. Several shelves are devoted to Niven's own works, which are a striking testimonial to the author's sixteen-year-career as a major science fiction talent. The living room, which is the scene of the interview, is visually enhanced by Niven's collection of light sculpture and Meerschaum pipes, many of which are priceless works of art.

This afternoon, Niven is casually dressed—dark slacks and a striped shirt. The author is average height and weight. His features are plain; his face shorn of distinguishing marks. Niven sports a nicely trimmed mustache and beard, modern horn-rimmed glasses, and a Meerschaum pipe, almost an appendage of the author. He is round-faced, endowed with dark wavy hair, and light in complexion. His voice is soft, quiet, restrained. His gestures and expressions are unemphatic, except, that is, when he is pressed on a particular point. In many ways, he gives the appearance of being almost "professorial" in attitude and demeanor, a natural first impression given his shyness and modesty.

Niven is a good talker—bright, articulate, engaging. His tone this afternoon is enthusiastic; he is unusually animated throughout the interview, obviously relishing the opportunity to express his views. He speaks in a measured, precise, direct manner. His words are devoid of anything unnecessary. Niven waits for a question to be asked, leans slightly backwards on the couch, draws a long puff on his pipe, and then responds with studied care to the inquiry. He answers all questions put to him. His responses are revealing and straightforward. Indeed, he wastes few words in zeroing in on a point. Overall, he reveals a wry wit, an engrossing presence, and an affable manner.

JE: From your perspective, can good science fiction writing be taught?

LN: There are some things that can be taught. There are some general rules to follow. You have to start with the ability to play with ideas for fun. If ideas don't excite you, you won't ever be a good science fiction writer. But the fact is, it's not enough just to have good stories to tell. You also have to know how to tell them. Technique is important, but it's something that can be learned.

JE: Do you think that science fiction writing is more difficult to teach than mainstream writing?

LN: Sure. You can't teach originality. Mainstream writers, generally, don't need originality. I'll give you a good example: *Lucifer's Hammer*. There's not much in the way of original thinking in that book. We did the research on comets, of course. We also did research on large meteor impacts. But from there, it was essentially mainstream, except for a few minor touches. It was simply a process of picking and choosing from the theories we had researched. And we always went with the most accepted theory. Most mainstream books, however, don't even get that original. They don't have to. They're presented simply as a slice of life. There's very little that's unique. Look at the spate of gothics, historicals, detectives, westerns, etc. In historicals, for instance, you don't want too many surprises. The writer tries to stay as close to historical fact as possible. Occasionally, he will weld two events together for plot purposes. And he'll usually say so in the accompanying notes. But originality? Original thinking would have Napoleon winning Waterloo by borrowing someone else's strategy worked out in World War II.

JE: If science fiction is, indeed, harder to write, then why is it viewed as such a despised genre by the literary establishment?

LN: The reader who buys a mainstream novel doesn't want any surprises. That's why he doesn't particularly like science fiction, which is riddled with surprises. In a mainstream novel, the reader wants to know what he's getting. And, generally, what he expects to get is a story in which the good guys win. Everything comes out happy ever after. The reader isn't interested in philosophical truths. Unfortunately, the pulp era produced some very negative attitudes toward science fiction. And the attitudes of the pulp era have hung on all these years. In truth, science fiction has changed a great deal since the pulps. It has become much more intelligent and engaging. It doesn't employ the trite plots which characterize mainstream novels. It's far richer in terms of ideas.

JE: One criticism made of science fiction by mainstream writers is that, unlike their work, science fiction characters are less complex, less developed, less real. Is that a fair assessment of the way that characterization is handled in most science fiction novels?

LN: I'm sure there are plenty of stories for which it's valid, although I don't think the charge can be made in such sweeping terms. Jerry Pournelle and I paid enormous attention to characterization, not only in *Lucifer's Hammer*, but also in *A Mote In God's Eye*, which is certainly science fiction. Basically, this attitude is another hang-over from the pulp era. It also fits the necessities of the genre. The originality, the new ideas, these are the important things in science fiction. In mainstream novels, think of a memorable character. He's certainly not the average man. A good example is *Arrowsmith*. Arrowsmith is no average doctor. If you look through the telephone book, you'll be hard-pressed to find a doctor like Arrowsmith, even if you try a thousand times. Arrowsmith is unusual, unique. In science fiction, though, if you use an unique or unusual character, then you're not really showing much about the society. The game in science fiction is to predict societies that might arise out of the present time. You need an average man embedded within the society if you want to say anything significant about its shape.

JE: Another criticism that's leveled at science fiction, both by its adherents as well as its detractors, is that the people who read science fiction aren't really interested in style and technique; that they read science fiction for its ideas as opposed to its literary value. Moreover, they maintain that science fiction readers are far less sophisticated, far less informed, and far less involved than their mainstream counterparts. How do you respond to that argument?

LN: Basically, I would respond by saying that it's none of my business. Anytime I get a question from an audience that seems to come from a total "fughead," I'll make approximately the following statement: "I, sir, do not write for everybody. I will pass your name around among the libraries and bookstores, and you will never be permitted to buy or read a Larry Niven book again. Reading Larry Niven is a privilege, not a right." Of course, it's a totally empty threat. What I'm telling you is that I don't get to pick my readers. The readers pick themselves. If there are "fugheads" reading my books, then that's not my fault. Furthermore, they paid the same price as the geniuses. If they don't like the way I write, then they'll quit buying my books. It's their choice.

JE: One of the major tasks of any science fiction writer is the ability to create future societies which are logical and believable. Is there a secret to doing that effectively?

LN: I don't know if I can answer that question. I've picked up a certain amount of knowledge, for example, in sociology. I try to work it into my stories wherever it's called for. However, I don't use it that much. When we first started working together, Jerry Pournelle told me that we couldn't work within the framework of my "Known Space" series; that he couldn't believe my social rules or the politics of my societies. I said, okay, we'll work in yours. And we did. I don't know how to teach anyone how to create a believable society. All I can tell him, I suppose, is that he'll learn it from reading good science fiction. And if he doesn't, he'll get lots of letters telling him what he did wrong.

JE: Some observers maintain that in order to write good science fiction, one must be well-versed in the social sciences as well as the physical sciences. Do you think that's a necessary requirement?

LN: Yes, very much so. You need both. I'll tell you this: the poets of the past, the ones who are remembered, poets like Pope, Dante, Kipling, are the ones who understood the sciences of their day. For example, you can discern a thorough knowledge of astrology and theology throughout Dante's work. Pope understood the atomic theory of his day. And Kipling understood the dynamics of engineering. He wrote some gripping poems about engineers. Today, a poet isn't expected to understand relativity. Well, he damn well should be! And, in fact, the people who would have been writing poetry today are writing science fiction instead. A good example is Chip Delany, who thinks of himself as a poet. Most science fiction writers don't think in those terms. But if you read them carefully, you'll find that their prose is quite poetic. Every so often, I'll experiment with poetry myself, even in a book I'm writing with Jerry Pournelle. In truth, Jerry can't do it too effectively, so he leaves it to me to weave in the telling phrases. Any good science fiction writer would make a good poet—better than most of the poets who are being published today.

JE: As a master of "hard" science fiction, how deep a knowledge of science does one need in order to write science fiction?

LN: Not very much. You don't need to know much science if you're writing in your area of expertise. My secret is that my area of expertise keeps growing. The first few stories I wrote were all within a relatively small area of expertise, mainly in the area of astrophysics. In order to develop greater expertise, I did considerable research in other areas. I looked things up when I had to. Nowadays, I know lots of people who tell me what's happening. I still subscribe to *Scientific American*, but I've also got Robert Forward's phone number. Forward is one of the foremost experts on gravity in the world. I read all the major publications, but I've also got some sane geniuses as well as some insane geniuses around. For instance, every Thursday I go to the Los Angeles Science Fantasy Society's meetings. And every so often, someone comes running in saying, "Hey, they've just discovered rings around Neptune," or some other such statement. And that's great! It keeps me right on the crest. You don't have to get that elaborate, though, to write science fiction, especially if you're a newcomer. Presumably, you've got an area of expertise. And if you don't, you can get it in a year. If you've got a story idea, it can always be researched. However, you can't make up your own laws of physics. That's the surest way to be laughed out of the field. A lot of non-science fiction readers have the idea that we make up our own scientific laws as we go along. Bullshit!

JE: How would you characterize, then, the kind of science fiction which Ray Bradbury writes? Do you even view it as science fiction?

LN: No. Ray Bradbury is a fantasy writer. He's never written science fiction. In fact, several years ago we discussed this question. He's perfectly aware of the distinction. He's never really claimed to write science fiction, at least not recently. His Mars was impossible at the time he wrote *The Martian Chronicles*. And I'm sure he knew it. Now, there's a man who's more of a poet than most writers and, in fact, more than the average science fiction writer. As you know, the basic rule of poetry is conciseness. Well, Bradbury's stories are so bloody concise that he's ruined a lot of new writers. He never really writes stories per se. He simply implies a story by writing the heart of it. It's an extremely difficult technique, but one which looks easy. As a result, lots of writers have broken their hearts trying to write like Ray. And it just doesn't work. I've never tried. I have more sense.

JE: A related criticism of science fiction is that it's essentially escapist fiction, whereas mainstream fiction has a didactic function—that is, it teaches the reader important truths. Does science fiction serve a similar function?

LN: Yes, very much so. However, they have it backwards. It's science fiction that teaches; mainstream just entertains. As I said earlier, science fiction stretches your mind. It teaches you to think in new terms. As a matter of fact, it's difficult to discuss science fiction as a genre because it's so diverse. However, all good science fiction reflects one basic attitude—namely, that there's someone out there who thinks as well as you do, but differently. Now, that's a hard message to get across, but one that's absolutely vital. Moreover, science fiction teaches tolerance. It forces you to get into the other guy's shoes for a moment, just to figure out what he's about. It teaches you never to criticize someone's intelligence until you know his motives. All of these lessons are learned by reading good science fiction.

JE: Can science fiction also expand the reader's horizons in terms of science?

LN: Certainly. The problem is, however, you have to pick your authors quite carefully. You have to read Larry Niven instead of Alan Dean Foster, or you have to read Robert Heinlein instead of Chip Delany. There are lots of people in the field who make up their own laws of physics. They don't try to hide that fact. And even they have a fairly good grasp of physics. It's just that they need some new invention or discovery a hundred years from now to make their stories work. Most science fiction writers, for instance, use the concept of faster-than-light travel. Most of us, however, are perfectly aware of the fact that presentday theory precludes it. Well, we say so! We don't hid the fact that it's impossible today. We simply assume a discovery sometime in the future.

JE: One of the things that you do well in your stories, I think, is that rather than employ fast talk or simplistic explanation in order to hurdle a difficult question, you make a concerted effort to explain the scientific issue involved. Are you ever tempted to short-circuit that process of careful reasoning?

LN: No. It's the thing I'm best at. And I'm well aware of it. Actually, I was quite good at it years ago. When I wrote "Neutron Star," I explained tides to the reader, which is damn difficult to get across, even for a physics teacher. And I did it in the context of dialogue in a story. I would hate to tell you how long I spent writing out that explanation and tearing it apart before I got it right. Fortunately, it worked!

JE: Since you're primarily viewed as a "hard" science fiction writer, does that pose any special requirements in terms of using science more extensively than you might otherwise?

LN: I'm tempted to laugh. There's a story I wrote, "For A Foggy Night," several years ago. The theory behind the story is that of alternate time tracks, coupled with the notion that sometimes time tracks merge. The visible sign of the merging is a thick fog. If you walk into a fog, you could easily wind up on another time line. Now, the typical response is, "Wait a minute, fog is caused by tiny water droplets surrounding it," to which my reply is, "Nonsense, everybody knows that water is transparent." Okay, it was a short story. It's tough to believe bullshit like that for more than twelve pages. And that's exactly how long the story was. But I'm not restricted to anything. I'm certainly not restricted to writing "hard" science stories. One of my first stories was a simple fantasy. It was a devil story, in which the central character got out of a bad bargain by forcing the demon to appear within a pentagram drawn on the demon's belly. Needless to say, the demon found it very difficult!

JE: As you see it, is trend-guessing an important part of science fiction writing?

LN: Yes, very much so. What isn't important, though, is that the writer get it right. As a science fiction writer, I'm not responsible for a change in a given trend. I simply pick the one that's most likely. Guessing at the future is something a science fiction writer may do better than the average man, but he's not expected to do it perfectly. In fact, if he did, all science fiction would have a depressing sameness. For example, when Frank Herbert's book, *Dune*, came out, and scored such a great success, all the science fiction stories of that period seemed to reflect an ecological basis. I think it's wise, however, for a science fiction writer to follow all possible trends, just to keep things interesting. As for me, I don't consider myself responsible if the scientific basis of a story goes wrong or gets disproved. It's not even annoying to me any longer. Every time they change the face of Mars, as a result of some new discovery, I simply write another story. That's why you get the peculiar situation in the *Tales of Known Space*, in which there are three Mars stories, each a sequel to the previous one, except that Mars itself keeps changing.

JE: Many people believe that science fiction is largely a product of the writer's imagination; that there's very little relationship between science fiction and real life. To what extent is your writing an outgrowth of your own life experiences?

LN: It shows itself mostly in terms of characterization. What I know of people, what they think and how they behave, is reflected in my stories. And, as I mentioned earlier, there are people out there who may think differently from you, but just as well. I try to anticipate how someone 500 years from now, in a given situation, will view the universe. As a result, you get the observations of Beowulf Shaefer, who is always lecturing the reader; who tells you that an Earthling tends to behave as if the universe were designed for him, whereas nobody on the other planets would make such a stupid assumption.

JE: In building new worlds and inventing new societies, do you ever find yourself engaging in polemics—that is, using your stories as a forum from which to espouse your own social and political views?

LN: No. I don't have that tendency. I've never been totally sure about any political assumption. There is, of course, some political and social commentary in my stories, but not a great deal. In fact, most of my characters don't even get involved in the politics of their day and know very little about it. That's certainly true of Beowulf Shaefer, Gil "The Arm" Hamilton, Louis Wu, and many others. Toss them into politics and they get totally bewildered. Actually, my characters don't even understand the politics of their day as well as I understand mine. And I don't understand very much.

JE: How do you anticipate, in writing science fiction, what humans in a distant world will be like; what they will think, how they will act, what they will value?

LN: I do the best I can. After all, I know something about people. I simply try to guess what truths, which are relevant today, will not be so in the future. A good example is the state of modern medicine. We're all very concerned if we get a pain in our appendix, experience violent fits of rage, or whatever. Well, I make the assumption that medicine will get much better in the next 500 years, just as it has gotten better in the last 500 years. The result of this progress will mean that no one will be plagued with a limp, no one will have to wear glasses, no one will be troubled by a toothache, etc. This view is expressed in my story, "Safe at Any Speed," which is set around 3300 A.D. Here, the main character never even worries about his car after it's been swallowed by a roc.

JE: As I listen to you speak, I hear you saying that if *you* can believe something, then it's probably believable. Do you write for an audience of Larry Nivens?

LN: Yes. The audience I have in mind when I write is a lot like me. I have to assume, though, that my reader is capable of the willing suspension of disbelief. And I'm obligated to strain that ability as little as possible. That's why I resort to so much explanation. For instance, if I'm going to use the trojan point concept, then I've got to tell the reader what that implies. Actually, the reader's suspension of disbelief is easier to handle if I just tell him the facts. That's another reason I tend to lecture so much in my stories. When I do lecture, though, I think I do it quite well. I rely on short sentences, coupled with pithy images.

JE: One problem in developing future socities, I suspect, is doing it in such a manner as to minimize unnecessary chaos. How do you go about reducing chaos, particularly when you're dealing with so many unknown factors?

LN: Let's face it: Minimizing chaos is unrealistic. The real world is teeming with chaos. Everyone is moving in uncertain directions. No future I can predict will be free of this uncertainty. You'll never find a human history in which everyone behaves alike, each in a predictable fashion. It's just not going to happen. Actually, the history line of the "Known Space" series is quite chaotic. It's as chaotic as the last thousand years of history. And it should be. A writer who tries to minimize chaos is missing the point; he's distorting reality!

JE: When you build new worlds, and the accompanying social, political, and economic structures, what process do you employ to acquire a working familiarity with the world you're creating?

LN: That's easy to answer: I think and I think and I think. Basically, I daydream a lot. I don't start writing until I know what's going on. And, of course, a story can take a long time to jell. In fact, a few of my Hugo-award-winning short stories took several years to complete. "Neutron Star," for example, was first written as an essay for a composition class in college, with a totally different hero. My story, "Inconstant Moon," sat three-quarters finished on my desk until Jerry Pournelle read it and told me what I was doing wrong. It was only then that I finished it.

JE: Is there a point at which the strange or alien can become too strange or alien, particularly in terms of maintaining interest and believability?

LN: Yes. It occurs when the reader can no longer empathize with the characters. I might consider myself handicapped in this regard, although perhaps not really. I can reach pretty far. A good example is *A World Out of Time*. There's only one character from our time in that story, and everyone else thinks quite unlike anyone that you or I would recognize as a human being.

JE: Many science fiction writers contend that, in the end, the primary objective of science fiction is to entertain. If that's so, how important is "message" in the context of your work?

LN: If I'm not doing a good job of entertaining the reader, then, obviously, I'm not going to reach anyone. As a result, entertainment is my primary objective. Of course, I have my own ideas of how the universe works. Obviously, these ideas are incorporated into my stories. But I don't concentrate too hard on message, usually. *Lucifer's Hammer* is an exception. Jerry Pournelle and I have strong ideas on space travel and atomic power plants, and anybody who reads that book will know it. Sure, I have things to say. They tend to work themselves into my stories whether I want them in there or not. But I try not to preach. I never try to write message stories with the objective of attempting to change the reader's thinking on some issue.

JE: Speaking of atomic power, what explains the widespread public opposition to the construction of new nuclear power plants, a movement which seems to be spreading throughout the country?

LN: Some people are afraid of height. Some people are afraid of closed places. Some people are afraid of darkness. Some people are afraid of radiation. It's this fear of an unseen death, I suspect, which seems to motivate these people. Actually, their fear is perfectly reasonable, given the way they view the world. But the fact is, people who spend all their time worrying about atomic power plants are ignoring many things which are much more likely to kill them. I recently came across an article in the newspaper, for instance, which listed various items in the order that they might kill somebody. It turns out that working in a coal mine is about as dangerous as smoking cigarettes, and both are hundreds of times more likely to kill somebody than an atomic power plant. People who cater to the fear of atomic power are, in my opinion, morally reprehensible. For example, I think Ralph Nader's pronouncement on the subject—namely, that plutonium is one of the most deadly substances around—is sheer stupidity. He couldn't have meant that. He's not, after all, a mental deficient. Anyone knows that botulism toxin is thousands of times more dangerous than plutonium, even if you ate a spoonful of it. A spoonful of plutonium is almost certain death, while the amount of botulism toxin it would take to kill you is barely enough to see. I think most people are bright enough to recognize that fact. But the thing is, you can see the effects of botulism toxin. You can see a can bulging when it's been on the shelf too long. And so you throw it out. If you don't, it will kill you. In the end, then, it's this fear of an unseen death, coupled with widespread ignorance and misinformation.

JE: One by-product of the feminist movement is the concern over the lack of strong heroines. Do you think that women are portrayed accurately in most science fiction books?

LN: I think so. Shall I say, up-front, that I resent anyone telling me what to write. I won't take that from editors and I sure won't take it from critics. If I need a good female character for a particular story, then I'll do my damndest to create her. If I don't, then I sure as hell won't shove her in just so somebody can say, "Hey, Larry Niven isn't a male chauvinist pig!"

JE: One of the subjects that you've written a great deal about, and which is a particular forte of yours, is the development of believable terminology. Do you think most science fiction writers do a skillful job of inventing such terminology?

LN: Yes. In fact, no one does it but science fiction writers. We're the only ones who need to. It's a skill that's absolutely restricted to people who write science fiction. I think science fiction writers are doing it better today than ever before. H. P. Lovecraft was among the first to push for words that sound alien, and he pushed quite hard. I'm much better at it today than I was when I first started writing. The alien words in *World of Ptaavs* started out as a list of nonsense words that I wrote in a math class when I should have been listening to the professor's lecture. After I put the list together, I crossed out those words which couldn't possibly be pronounced. That list was incorporated into *World of Ptaavs*, "The Warriors," and other works. I spend much more time on it now, though. I also have a better grasp of what's going on. Consider the word, "newstaper." Now, that's a word with a host of implications. It not only tells you virtually everything about the guy's profession, but it also tells you that there are no more newspapers. Otherwise, such a word wouldn't be necessary.

JE: You're obviously a treasure chest of potential story ideas, many more than could ever be used. What determines whether you actually decide to write a story?

LN: When the idea jells into a story. When it does, I'm ready to write it. If it doesn't, then I'll spend some additional time mulling it over in my mind. Sometimes, Jerry Pournelle and I get together, armed with plenty of brandy and coffee, and try to see what we can come up with. I can't tell you when I'm ready to write a story. I can tell you that if a story isn't in my head, if I don't have an ending for it, then I'm not going to write it, at least not then. It's also true, though, that the ending I have in mind when I start the story might not be the final ending that's published. However, I must have some ending in mind before I sit down to write.

JE: How important is it to be topical in science fiction?

LN: Being topical is extremely important: I avoid it at all costs. A topical story is exactly the type of story that will be obsolete in a year. Only a damn fool writes topical stories.

JE: What hopes do you have for your work in terms of impact?

LN: Unless I think that people will be moved by a story, I won't bother to write it. I try to make my stories as interesting as possible. But impact isn't everything, at least immediate impact. Let me give you an example: *Close Encounters of the Third Kind*. The movie clearly has impact. You can't help but be enthralled by the movie. You walk out of the theatre feeling wonderful because aliens turn out to be such nice guys. Once you think about it for ten minutes, though, the whole plot melts in your hand, like a Hershey bar on a hot day. What there is of a plot, and there isn't very damn much, is unbelievable and unrealistic. I want my stories to have impact when they're read, but I'm more concerned with their being remembered, with their working on the reader's head. I would like the reader to go on thinking about them long after he has put the stories down. That's real impact, at least the kind I want.

JE: Do you find that writing science fiction serves a cathartic value for you—that is, does it teach you important things about yourself—your views, your feelings, your motivations?

LN: Yes. In fact, this is one of the best jobs in the world for precisely that reason. A writer psychoanalyzes himself, not with a psychiatrist, but with tens of thousands, hundreds of thousands, or maybe millions of readers. And these readers will never accuse him of fantasizing when he's dealing with what he thinks is reality, will accept any lie he wishes to tell about himself. I don't know Robert E. Howard, but he was probably quite different from Conan the Barbarian, and nobody was ever going to tell him so. No one cares. And furthermore, readers are paying large sums of money to be able to listen to you, which saves you the trouble and expense of having to pay a psychiatrist $50 an hour for the same privilege.

JE: In the course of writing, do you ever identify with the characters you've created?

LN: Sure. It was a tearing experience writing *Inferno*. Jerry Pournelle and I wrote *Inferno* in four months. We couldn't stop writing. It was a horrifying world in which to live. We had to get our characters out of there as quickly as possible. It was downright ugly in spots. We just couldn't stop moving.

JE: When you've written as many big books as you have, does that impose any special pressure when it comes to writing your next book?

LN: I suppose you can't help but feel that everyone out there is wondering what you're going to do for an encore. It's hard to avoid that feeling, but I don't let it bother me. The trick is to not let your success stop you from writing a story simply because it's fun. I've written a number of short stories recently, several of which were quite light-hearted. I don't feel any obligation to be profound. I'm not doing anything for an encore. And anybody who doesn't like what I write is perfectly free to stop buying my books or wait for the reviews to come out. That's really the most sensible approach anyway. I depend very much on the reviewers to tell me what a book is like before I go out and buy it. I would invite anyone who is disturbed by the variety of my books to simply wait and see what the reviewers have to say.

JE: What about the pressures you impose on yourself? For example, do you feel a need to achieve a higher and higher standard with each new book?

LN: No, that's not a real problem. I wouldn't write a sloppy story, anyway. Why should I bother? After all, I have a reputation to protect. I've never written a sloppy story, not by my standards. It's just that my standards keep changing. Every story I've written was the best I could do at the time. Obviously, there are some stories I'm disappointed in now, that I wish I had waited to write. However, even these stories were the best I could do when I wrote them.

JE: With the tremendous success you've achieved in the science fiction field, have you ever been tempted to try your hand at other literary genres?

LN: Sure. *Lucifer's Hammer* was quite different from anything I had ever done before. In fact, each of the three books I've done with Jerry Pournelle has been quite different from anything either of us had done before. Unless that's true, there's no reason to collaborate on a project. Collaborating is much too difficult to try unless there's a story you wish to tell, but which you can't write yourself. Every so often, though, I'll try to write something simply because I've never done it before. Once upon a time, it was a television script. Another time it was a collaboration with David Gerrold. Still, another time, it was creating a unique character who never moved a muscle. I like to try new things, but only if I think they'll make a good story. I'm not interested in experimentation for experimentation-sake.

JE: Are you an extremely ambitious person? Do you continuously set new goals for yourself?

LN: Yes, very much so. I'm not one who likes to rest on his laurels. On the other hand, I also do a lot of goofing off. I don't spend all of my time at the typewriter. For instance, I recently completed a fifty-mile hike with Jerry Pournelle and a group of Boy Scouts. There were eighteen of us in all. We went up hill and down dale, through hail storms and the like in the High Sierra. I also spend a lot of time reading for fun. I'm not a work-a-holic, but I like to get stories finished. For me, the best moment always comes when I know the story is perfect.

JE: Finally, many people wonder, I'm sure, why you push yourself so hard, particularly since it's not really a question of money. Why do you work so hard?

LN: I suppose you're referring to the fact that I was born with a trust fund, and would not have had to worry about money for the rest of my life. And that's true, of course. But if you think that's good enough for members of the Doheny family, then you're way off base. If I go to a party and someone asks me what I do, then I'd better damn well have an answer or no one's going to talk to me. I've now been writing for sixteen years, but I can certainly remember what it felt like. The fact is, people who belong to rich families must have a profession anyway or else. Nobody is a playboy these days. Nobody rejects the idea of working for a living simply because he's an aristocrat. In fact, the guy who doesn't do something for a living isn't going to have anything to talk about. Nobody will ever ask his philosophy of life, because what has he done to earn it? I started writing, partly, because I had run out of options. I now write because I like it, but also because I like the rewards. I like talking about story ideas with people. In fact, a lot of story ideas have come from people I know. For example, the "Alderson drive" in *A Mote In God's Eye* was suggested by Dan Alderson, a good friend of mine. I also like the involvement entailed with being a writer. I recently participated in a panel on what should go into the *Ringworld Engineers*. That was a fun experience. I also like to sign authographs. I like to get fan letters. I also like people to tell me what's wrong with my stories, and I like to prove them wrong or admit that they're right. It's all great fun!

RAY BRADBURY:

Poet of Fantastic Fiction

Corralling Ray Bradbury for an interview is, in an analogical sense, very much like lassoing a bucking bronco—it is an act which requires Herculean skill, inestimable patience, and lightning reflexes. Indeed, Bradbury's career these days resembles something akin to a live tornado. As he puts it, "I'm quietly going bats trying to finish a new book of poetry, a novel, and work on a play, as well as doing my work for Disney on EPCOT (their 'City of the Future') and keep up with all the lecture commitments I have." When I last spoke to Bradbury, he informed me that things had really closed in on him; NBC has given the final go-ahead for a six-hour mini-series on *The Martian Chronicles*, and he is currently planning to take the play on the road, where it will eventually find its way to New York, via numerous colleges and universities.

Despite his enormous success, Ray Bradbury has maintained a healthy perspective, observing, "I write for fun. You can't get too serious. I don't pontificate in my work. I have fun with ideas. I play with them. I approach my craft with enthusiasm and respect. If my work sparks a serious thought, fine. But I don't write with that in mind. I'm not a serious person. And I don't like serious people. I don't see myself as a philosopher. That's terribly boring. I want to shun that role. My goal is to entertain myself and others. Hopefully, that will prevent me from taking myself too seriously."

Ray Bradbury was born in Waukegan, Illinois, on August 22, 1920, but spent much of his childhood in Los Angeles, where he developed his skills as a writer. Each year his list of credentials increases by geometric proportions. He has been dubbed the most "anthologized" short story writer in the world today, with hundreds of new pieces coming out annually, in a wide variety of books and magazines. He has authored over two dozen volumes, many of which have become classics in the science fiction field. These include such best-selling works as: *The Martian Chronicles, Fahrenheit 451, Dandelion Wine, The Illustrated Man, Something Wicked This Way Comes, The October Country*, and numerous others. Two of his books, *Fahrenheit 451* and *The Illustrated Man*, have been made into feature movies.

As objective as one tries to be, there is something extraordinary about Ray Bradbury. He is more of everything in the flesh than he is in his books. A man of rare wit, energy, and drive, Bradbury lives as he writes—with style, and gusto, and daring. It is impossible to capsule Ray Bradbury in a few words.

He is a man of enormous talent, effervescent personality, and extraordinary vitality. He is blessed with an analytical mind, a fertile imagination, and an ability to translate thought into action. Bradbury is a superb conversationalist. He speaks with passion and verve; his words teem with drama and poetry. His sentences are punctuated with lyric notes—the words of the prophets, the teachings of the masters, the spirits of the muses. Bradbury delights in giving meaning and purpose to his words; they flow with style and grace. He is a romantic, a visionary, an aesthetic. He speaks a thousand tongues; his renaissance voice touches young and old, black and white, rich and poor. He is a man with a mission, one who endeavors to spread joy and happiness as far as the eye can see. And from the looks of it, he is doing a damn good job!

The following interview takes place at Bradbury's cavernous sixth-floor office on Wilshire Boulevard in the heart of Beverly Hills, California. His office, like his life, is chaotic; a frenzy of dialogue and activity. Here, amid piles of clutter and memorabilia, Bradbury pounds the typewriter keys with impish delight, giving vent to his galactic imagination. This afternoon, his conversation is thoughtful, engrossing, optimistic; a perfect blend of head and heart. During the course of the session, Bradbury discusses a host of topics—his philosophy of life, his interest in the arts, his attitudes about popular literature, his feelings about television, and a variety of other intriguing subjects.

JE: By your own admission, you write both science fiction and fantasy. What do you see as the basic difference between the two genres?

RB: Science fiction is the art of the possible. There's never anything fantastic about science fiction. It's always based on the laws of physics; on those things that can absolutely come to pass. Fantasy, on the other hand, is always the art of the impossible. It goes against all the laws of physics. When you write about invisible men, or walking through walls, or magic carpets, you're dealing with the impossible. Science fiction has a long history which goes back to the cavemen. Plato's book, *The Republic*, is a good example of science fiction. Everything starts in the head and then moves out into the world. Whenever you create something in the head first, you're writing science fiction. The history of science fiction is the history of ideas that have been laughed at. These same ideas are then born in fact and later change the world.

JE: In terms of your own experience, which of the two genres do you prefer?

RB: I don't really have a preference. I love to do everything. If a fantasy idea excites me, then I'll do it. If a science fiction idea excites me, then I'll do that. I never plan ahead. Everything is always spontaneous and passionate. I never sit down and think things out. I also do a great deal of daydreaming. Oh, I do some thinking in-between, but it's a very loose thing. I'm not super-intellectual. If it feels right, then I'll do it. I'll give you a good example of how ideas come to me. The other night I was in a local bookstore when a stranger came up and started to talk. He told me that he wanted to be a poet. We began to discuss football, when he remarked what a shame it was that they couldn't invent a machine that would suck in all the energy that goes into football and apply it to curing cancer. Well, I thought that was a grand idea! I asked him if I could have it, and he said, 'yes.' I'll probably do a poem on it, or perhaps a short story, or even a novel.

JE: One journalist attributes your interest in both of these literary forms to your boyhood experiences with carnivals and circuses. In what ways did they affect your decision to become a writer?

RB: I'm a product of many art forms. Thank God, I had a mother who was madly in love with movies. She started taking me to all sorts of fantastic films when I was three, beginning with *The Hunchback of Notre Dame*. Along the way, I went to a lot of magic shows. Once I even jumped up on stage and helped Blackstone with his act. When I was nine, I began to collect comic strips—"Buck Rogers," "Flash Gordon," "Tarzan." About that time, I started to hang around circuses and carnivals. I struck up a great friendship with a man named "Mr. Electrico," who really impressed me. I think that it was his influence which really encouraged me to become a writer. After we had several long talks, I went out and bought a typewriter and started writing. I've never stopped writing since then.

JE: In addition to those early life experiences, which writers have most influenced your own growth and development?

RB: Oh, that's hard. There are many of them; each one has affected me in a different way at a different time. A lot of women writers have influenced me—Eudora Welty, Edith Wharton, Katherine Anne Porter, Ellen Glasgow, Jessamyn West. Other writers like Ernest Hemingway, Thomas Wolfe, John Steinbeck, and William Faulkner have taught me a great deal. I've also been influenced by writers like George Bernard Shaw, William Shakespeare, Gerard Manley Hopkins, Alexander Pope, and G. K. Chesterton. There's no one around today, however, who really impresses me.

JE: One writer said of your early work, "He did not cease to be a teacher when he stopped writing science fiction, but he did place a moratorium on the more evangelistic kind of moralizing which he was practicing in the 1940s and early 1950s." As you look back on your career, did you often moralize in your early work?

RB: Oh, I'm sure I did. I still do. It's important, however, to do it as subtly as possible. You don't want to be a bore about it. That was the nice thing about George Bernard Shaw. He could moralize, but turn it into a lot of fun. He was always making one point or another. But he was never so serious that he spoiled the fun. I suppose that's why my book, *Fahrenheit 451*, is still around. While I was making serious points, I also wrote a good suspense novel. The novel was so good, that you had to put up with the moralizing.

JE: What is the relationship, as you see it, between art and propaganda?

RB: Well, since we're all a part of life, I don't see how it's possible not to propagandize. We all have strong feelings about certain things—love, sex, war, politics. These things should be the mainstays of one's art. They're an integral part of life. They can't be separated from art.

JE: In 1962, you remarked, "We must seek ways to know and encourage the good in ourselves, the will toward life." How have you attempted to achieve that goal in your own life?

RB: As best you can, you attempt to set an example that will help you to know yourself and others. That means you must be totally honest with yourself, particularly about your destructive impulses. You must learn to face up to them in yourself. If you can do that, the people around you will be much more forgiving of your mistakes.

JE: In a recent article, you argued that all arts, big and small, should aim toward "the elimination of wasted motion in favor of concise declaration."

What did you mean by that statement?

RB: In order to be a good writer, you must first explode passionately and then render it down. It's always best to do the big thing initially, and then cut it down to size. Every time I write a short story, I'll do about thirty pages and then pare it down to around twenty pages. The important thing is getting it out and not thinking about it. I've seen more good ideas ruined by people thinking about them instead of doing them. When you're writing something, don't think about it, just do it!

JE: Generally speaking, you've received extremely good reviews from the critics. What do you see as the proper role of a critic?

RB: Whenever I'm asked to review a book, I never do so unless I really like it. I don't see my job as trying to destroy the book. Unfortunately, there are many critics who enjoy that role. I only pick those books that I'm super-enthused about, and then try to sell them to people. I want them to share my loves, not my hates.

JE: Do you care greatly about the critics? Are you concerned with their views?

RB: I don't give a damn about the critics. I'm not interested in what they have to say. Really, I don't care about other people's opinions. If I did, I wouldn't have any career at all. I've been warned time and time again not to write science fiction by my friends, my teachers, and all the great intellectuals of our time. That's what's wrong with our culture. Too many people listen to what other people have to say. Who cares? Don't look to others for guidance. Look to yourself! That's what's great about science fiction. Every writer in the science fiction world is a different kind of writer. We all have different views of the world. Some of us are conservatives. Others are liberals. We all know each other. And we respect each other. We all get along. And we do very little fighting. There's plenty of room for Arthur Clarke, who writes one way, and Robert Heinlein, who writes another way. We don't look over each other's shoulder for approval. We each do our own thing.

JE: Some time ago, you expressed the view that the American novel was bankrupt of idea, style, and imagination on any level. Why do you think that's true?

RB: I don't know. You have the "New York Mafia" which rolls logs for each other—people like John Updike, Philip Roth, Norman Mailer. It's a very insular thing. It's also extremely intellectual, which makes it very dangerous. I suppose it's inevitable that there must be some type of conflict between the people who think and the people who feel. The truth is, not one of these writers would know a good idea if it came up and bit him. Updike is all style and no idea. It's amazing how little this man thinks. It's unfortunate that these writers receive so much attention. Look at Mailer and the publicity he received from his book on graffiti. I thought it was a ridiculous book. Whether he knows it or not, graffiti isn't beautiful; it's ugly. If we're not careful, it will destroy our cities. Come on, that's a lousy idea!

JE: Several times you've referred to the one-dimensional nature of the intellectual, of his inability to think and feel at the same time. What lies at the heart of the problem?

RB: I'm not sure. After all, ideas can be lots of fun. The intellect is a great game. Some of the most enjoyable evenings of my life have been spent with bright friends in the science fiction field. We would get an idea, throw it up in the air, and create with it. It's like a lot of kids playing basketball. You're all over the court, throwing the ball around, scoring points from all directions. There are some writers, however, who had this quality. Gerald Heard had it. Bertrand Russell had it. Aldous Huxley had it. When you met them, they were like bright children. They could be serious, but they also had a wonderful sense of humor.

JE: Throughout your life, you've had a love affair with books. With so many people turned off to reading, how did you develop such a keen interest in books?

RB: I found in books the romance and ideas on which to feed. I was really quite a glutton. I used to memorize entire books. I suppose that's where the ending of *Fahrenheit 451* comes from—where the book people wander through the wilderness and each of them is a book. That was me when I was ten. I was *Tarzan of the Apes*. I used to love all of Edgar Rice Burroughs' books. I've always enjoyed the smell of books. If you don't have that primitive feeling about books to begin with, I don't think you'll ever make it as a writer. I've kept up my acquaintance with children's books throughout the years. All of my books, really, are children's books. I don't write books only for grown-ups. I just write books. Now, they're passing them from one generation to another. I'm so proud to be sharing the shelves with my real heroes—Jules Verne, H. G. Wells, Robert Louis Stevenson, Nathaniel Hawthorne, Edgar Allan Poe. All of their books have somehow found their way into the hands of children. As for libraries, they're great places. I can't stay away from them. I had to educate myself after I left high school. I used to take home ten books at a time. I read every book I could find on writing. I also got into philosophy, religion, music, art, and poetry. I've educated myself in virtually every art form that exists.

JE: Obviously, you enjoy being a writer. What about that lifestyle most agrees with you?

RB: I'm not sure that I have a particular lifestyle. I've been extremely lucky to have a good family and raise four lovely daughters. My daughters are all film enthusiasts, so it has been relatively easy for me to share a lot of my loves with them. I never get bored with life. I don't let myself get into a rut. Writers are fortunate because they can shift gears more easily than the average person. I have continually put myself in a position to fail so that I could become a student again. It has taken me thirty-five years to learn to write poetry. And that has been lots of fun. In fact, it has kept me alive at times. I rarely get depressed. Whenever I feel down, I walk away and do something else. I find that writing is still a challenge. I'm experimenting more with novels. I'm also learning to write screenplays. Recently, I've been getting more and more into music.

JE: On your office door, there's a sign stating that you're a working writer—that you arrive at nine o'clock and leave at four o'clock. Do you start each day with the idea of writing a fixed number of pages, or do you take the view that whatever happens, happens?

RB: Basically, I just go in with the idea of writing something. I usually start off the day with poetry. I go through a process of free association. I do the same thing with short stories. A lot of my best poetry has come from just sitting down at the typewriter and thinking up some crazy line. As far as work goes, once I've done four good pages, then I'll let myself off for the rest of the day, unless it's going extremely well. If that's the case, I might work until the piece is finished. I think that the work a person does in a single day is very important. In many ways, writing a novel resembles a segmented worm. Each day you're a different person. By the time you've reached the end of a novel, you're much different from when you started. In fact, you can have 365 different novels on your hands unless you're careful. If I'm writing a novel, I try to finish it within nine days. Otherwise, it will usually bog down, become overly intellectual, and lose its fun.

JE: Are you a rapid writer? Do words come easily to you?

RB: Yes, especially now. It didn't use to be that way. When I first started out, I was able to write fairly rapidly, but it was usually lousy. That's the thing it's difficult to get students to understand. If I were teaching the short story in high school, for instance, I wouldn't be interested in quality at all. I'd be interested in product. I'd just want them to do it. And then I'd pat them on the head. If they did something extraordinary, I'd say, "Wow, that's great!" I'd correct their grammar. And I'd make them do their stories over again until they got it. Really, I'd want quantity, which, in the end, would guarantee quality. Then you can begin to criticize kids when they reach nineteen, twenty, twenty-one years old. Before that, you run the risk of damaging them. I'd just want the work, that's all.

JE: Are there some genres that you feel more comfortable with than others?

RB: No, not really. They're all getting easier now. Poetry was rough for awhile. Now, I'm getting better at it. I'll give you an idea of the way these things happen. The editor of *Pro Football* magazine got in touch with me several years ago and said, "We want you to write an essay on football for our magazine." I said, "That's ridiculous! Why did you ask me? I don't write that sort of thing." I thanked him for thinking of me, and hung up the phone. Then I got to thinking about my last year in high school, the weather, the smell of leaves, the football games. I went to all the football games that last year, and fell in love with the sport. The more I thought about it, the more I got to like the idea. And so I sat down, and in seven minutes, I wrote an eight-page poem about football, entitled, "All Flesh Is One." Jesus, I looked at it after I'd finished it, and it was the first poem I'd written in my life that I really liked. God, it was good! And I called the guy back and said, "Guess what, I've got something for you, but I don't think you're going to like it. It's a poem. I know you don't print poems. I realize that people don't go to a Ram's game to read poetry." "Well," he said, "send it to me and I'll take a look at it." So I sent it to him. And, you know, I got the fastest acceptance I've ever had in my life. He sent me a check for $400, which is an incredible amount, especially for poetry. You're usually lucky to get $10. And he also sent me a letter, which was even more important to me, in which he said, "I'm sending your poem to my father. He loves football!" Well, it was published in the magazine, and later used on the cover. The whole thing was accidental. I went with the emotion. That's why, when you feel something, go do it!

JE: In a recent article, Russell Kirk said of you, "For like C. S. Lewis and J. R. R. Tolkien, Ray Bradbury has drawn his sword against the dreary and corrupting materialism of this century." Is this how you picture yourself, and, if so, how does this translate in terms of your writing?

RB: Yes, I think he's right in many ways. I would add to that, I also draw the sword at cliche answers. It's so easy, for example, to say, "Oh, we're becoming computerized. All machines are bad. We're becoming robots." Well, that's partially true, but not completely true. Not all technology is bad. Whenever intellectuals become too critical of machines, I like to ask them to consider those machines which serve to humanize life—for instance, motion picture projectors, record players, television sets, etc. These things help to enlarge life by repeating truths over and over. They make us prize our existence. We hope they will accumulate in the blood. Before we conclude that all machines are bad, we must consider the totality of machines. We have to be fair. Those machines that don't work need to be redesigned. The automobile is a machine that doesn't work very well. So we must redesign it. We must make it safer, more economical, less polluting. We must learn to humanize the machine. Machines must be made to embody humanistic principles. We must design them that way. They must reflect our moral concerns. Then it becomes a question of how they're used, of what we do with them. That's up to us!

JE: One critic of yours remarked, "The problem with Ray Bradbury is that he never grew up." How do you respond to that charge?

RB: That's nice! I like to hear that. I certainly hope not. What is growing up, anyway? I remember discussing this question when I was in Italy several years ago. A friend of mine said he doubted if anyone ever grew up. I wasn't really sure at the time. Now that I'm older, I realize he was right. If you grow up the way most people think you should, then you're bound to be a real danger to society. Life can't be taken seriously. I agree with Mark Twain on that. You have to have a sense of humor. You have to remain a child for your whole life, or else life isn't worth living. If you lose your sense of fun, what's left?

JE: In recent speeches, you've discussed religion and the role it has played in your life. How has it influenced your thought?

RB: The problem of Christianity is finding new language for the old symbols. The mystery is still there. We pretend it isn't, but it's there. There's no dichotomy between science and theology. It's a made-up dichotomy. They both deal with the same mystery. And they're both ignorant. We need the two ignorances in order to survive. The scientist has an ignorance called "theory." There's nothing to substantiate it. It's merely that. It's faith in the unknown. It's untested fact. But the facts can't really be explained. That's where the theologians take over with the other half of the ignorance. And since we're ignorant, we need something to go on besides the facts.

JE: Do you still consider yourself a science fiction writer, or do you view yourself more now as simply a fiction writer?

RB: I'm an idea writer. Everything of mine is permeated with my love of ideas—both big and small. It doesn't matter what it is as long as it grabs me, and holds me, and fascinates me. And then I'll run out and do something about it. My poetry, all of it, is idea poetry. That's not true for all poetry. Very specific ideas hit me, and I say to myself, "Oh, no one has ever written a poem on that before," and so I'll do it. Let me give you an example—take the relationship between Shakespeare and Melville. A few years ago, while doing research on Melville's life, I discovered that he had never read Shakespeare until he was thirty years old. He was busy writing a book about whales; how to kill whales, how to render down their blubber, etc. He was writing a history of whaling of sorts. One day, Melville went off to Boston and came across a set of Shakespeare, seven volumes in large type. He took it home and read it, after which he took his whaling book and threw it out the window. In the next seven months, lo and behold, out of his brow, out of his soul, Shakespeare called him and said, "Oh, Herman Melville, truly come ye forth and birth yourself in whale." And that's what happened. This giant whale slid right out of his head, inspired by

Shakespeare and his love for Hamlet, King Lear, Richard III, Othello, and others. Out of this collision of souls, so to speak, came *Moby Dick*. That's a fabulous encounter, isn't it? Well, I couldn't resist writing a long poem about it. And it's one of my best poems. It's in my new collection.

JE: Does writing science fiction today pose the same challenge and excitement that it did when you started out in the field?

RB: Oh God, yes! In fact, it's more exciting today. A lot of my poetry is science fiction poetry. My new play, *The Martian Chronicles*, has been extremely satisfying. I'm older now, my enthusiasm is high, and I'm trying to find new ways of understanding my younger self. And so, my new plays, my science fiction plays, represent a new level of consciousness. For instance, I've taken the *Moby Dick* mythology and transferred it to outer space. I've also done a play entitled, *Leviathan 99*, which was totally influenced by *Moby Dick*. In fact, I dedicated the play to Herman Melville. It's a long poem, actually. While the concept belongs to Melville, the language is mine. This project excited me as much as writing *The Martian Chronicles*, which I did nearly thirty years ago.

JE: Are you generally pleased with the quality of science fiction writing today?

RB: In reality, the problem has remained essentially the same. Nothing really gets better. There's always a small handful of talented writers who do good work in any particular age, and all the rest are merely adequate. That's true for science fiction as well. Thirty-five years ago, we had, roughly speaking, a dozen or so, really fine science fiction writers. There were another twenty to thirty who were good. And there were twenty to thirty more who were fair. That's still the case today. There's a lot of good people working today, many of whom were around twenty or thirty years ago—people like Robert Heinlein, Arthur Clarke, Theodore Sturgeon, and the like. Moreover, there are many new writers coming into the field, with a great love for it. I don't think, though, that there's been any huge change in quality. It's pretty much the same situation, with about twelve to fourteen people doing the bulk of the good writing.

JE: Do you see science fiction, as a genre, moving in any new directions in the foreseeable future?

RB: I suspect we'll move more into philosophy, more into theology, at least I think so. The further we go into space, the more we're going to be awed and terrified by our lonely position in the universe. That means we'll need to do a lot of thinking about the future, which is what I'm trying to do with my poetry. I want to help us to explain ourselves to ourselves. That has always been a constant in science fiction, but I think it will dominate our thinking in the next forty years.

JE: There's considerable disagreement over what makes for good science fiction. Are there any special qualities which distinguish science fiction from other literary genres?

RB: No. The same attributes that characterize fiction writing in any field are equally true for science fiction—namely, observation and truth. For instance, if you read the book, *The Virginian*, which is a chronicle of the early west, you can't help but say to yourself, "My God, what a great writer this man is!" Or in the area of portraying middle class life and customs, read some of Ring Lardner's books. He was a genius at characterization. Or in the field of humor, take a look at Robert Benchley or Stephen Leacock. You'll laugh your head off! However, the reason you're laughing your head off is because it's true. Its a fantastic stretching of reality, so that we can swallow it and let out a roar. Science fiction is very much the same thing. *The Martian Chronicles* is a metaphor for a way of viewing the universe, of viewing our planet and the other planets. It works because it rings a bell of truth. It looks like a fantasy, but it isn't. It will only work if you, the reader, feel that the writer has an honest way of looking at the world. You can apply that standard to Robert Heinlein or Arthur Clarke or Theodore Sturgeon. It has held true over time, whether you're talking about fiction or non-fiction.

JE: What accounts for the short supply of good writers in America today?

RB: That's a tough one. The short story has certainly languished, hasn't it? Even the biggest writers rarely do short stories. I suppose that television is part of the problem. More and more writers are going into television. They see it as much easier work. However, you can't learn writing by writing for television. There's no real writing in the average script. Many of these writers are enticed by the big money that television offers. Money has never really been a driving motivation in my life. I've been glad when it showed up, but for many years, I was smart enough to stick to my loves, even when it meant thirty or forty dollars a week. That continued until I was twenty-nine or thirty. My wife even had to work to support us when we were first married.

JE: Speaking of television, are you a fan of any particular program?

RB: Sure. The really good writing takes place in the comedy end of television. There are very few people who write good drama. The comedy shows, however, are usually witty and amusing. They may not be super-great, but I couldn't write them. I admire that kind of excellence when it occurs. A good example that comes to mind is the show, *M*A*S*H*.

JE: Have you ever aspired to be a performer?

RB: Yes. In fact, when I started out, I was an actor. I did a lot of theatre work until I was twenty. It was great fun to perform. That's one reason why I stay in the theatre. It's certainly not for the money. None of my plays, with the exception of *The Martian Chronicles*, have ever made a dime, and that's after forty-five years in the theatre. I suppose that's why I lecture as much as I do. It gives me a good opportunity to perform. I'll usually do scenes from some of my plays, or perhaps read some of my poetry. I enjoy the feeling of being in front of an audience.

JE: What do you see as the secret of your enormous staying power as a writer?

RB: As I look back over my life, everything I've done has been exactly right for me. When I left high school, we were very poor. In fact, we were on relief when I graduated. We had few prospects for the future. It was 1938, and there were nearly fifteen million people unemployed. I was never very education-oriented. However, I was always very doing-oriented. I knew how to gravitate toward people who could teach me something. I've always had a good relationship with English teachers, drama instructors, vocal teachers, professional librarians, book people, etc. When I graduated from high school, I formed an *ad hoc* study group. We met every night at someone's house for the next year. That became our college. And a damn good one! Then I got into a science fiction group. I met Henry Kuttner and Robert Heinlein. It was a one-to-one relationship. The more teachers you can have as friends, the more you'll be able to grow as a person. I've seen it happen over and over. As for my success, I suppose it's this whole thing of ideas. You can take a short story idea of mine and you can write your own short story based on that idea. I seem to have the ability of finding metaphors that are so engaging, so sharp, so telling, so poetic, that you—the reader—are tempted to write a variation on it. I'll give you a good example: my short story, "There Will Come Soft Rains." It's the story of a mechanized house in the future, one that goes on living and breathing long after the inhabitants have gone away. You can give that idea to a bunch of kids in elementary school or junior high school or high school, and say, "Write your own version of the story. What would your house be like? How would you build it? What would you put in it?" Well, that's a fun idea, isn't it? I suppose that's why my stories are popular; why I can get people to come to my lectures. I'll shift in and out of these ideas. I'll apply them in poetry one moment; then I'll do a play about them the next moment; then I'll do a short story about them the next moment; then I'll do an essay about them the next moment; then I'll do a screenplay about them the next moment; and so on. I'm all over the place. I never stop moving. I suspect there's an attraction in that.

JE: Finally, as you look at the state of the world today, are you optimistic about the future, both its prospects and challenges?

RB: There are two sides to the coin. I'm an optimist insofar as individuals are concerned, and a pessimist when it comes to groups. The more we can break things down and get them into the hands of individuals, the more likely we'll be able to solve our problems. I'm an optimist when it comes to me, because I know I can solve problems. I've done it. I've got my whole life behind me to make me optimistic about my future. I'm a total optimist on that count. As I see it, there must always be a "madman" in charge of a group to make it work; otherwise, it never comes off. People get tired and give up. The madman is someone who's a little bit crazy, but who also has a sense of humor, which enables people to excuse him for being bright. But the more I see of groups, the more I think that every group needs a madman—a benevolent Ahab. Every so often, in politics, for example, a madman comes along who can get things done. Someone like President Truman was a tremendous self-starter. He had the ability to make things happen. But today, all the labels have changed. We don't know what we are anymore. We're living in a period of "radical conservatism," which is something we've needed for a long time. It's not the conservatism of a William Buckley, but more like that of Albert Knox. It's the person who says, "Power to the people!" That's what Angela Davis is all about. She's not a liberal. She's a radical conservative. The liberals believe in spending more money and giving more power to big government. We've discovered that doesn't work. Money doesn't solve problems. Imagination does! Enthusiasm does! You can pour all the money you want into education, but unless you have a madman in the classroom to teach, you won't do the job. I'm optimistic because I see people, like Ralph Nader and others, who are trying to regain power from the central government. We need town halls again. We need to break down the cities. We need local control. Basically, I see a trend in this direction, which makes me optimistic. I think we'll make it. It's simply a question of applying ourselves. We need to turn inward a bit and concentrate on solving those problems which confront us.

A. E. VAN VOGT:

A Writer with a Winning Formula

There are few science fiction writers alive today who can boast the singular achievements of A. E. van Vogt, a long-time talent in the field, who has spent his lifetime giving meaning and import to the shape of things to come. Most at home with books and ideas, van Vogt prizes the gifts of reason and logic, and uses them to solve life's myriad puzzles. Clearly, van Vogt personifies the mysteries and vagaries of the human intellect, a fact which is reflected in everything he says and does.

A. E. van Vogt is a problem-solver par excellence. Nothing excites him more than inventing a "system" to solve a vexing dilemma. Although many science fiction critics view him as a "traditionalist," his writing reflects a deep love for the "experimental." This concern is evidenced in his life as well, which reveals a man who delights in invention. Indeed, he has studied the machinations of violence, employed the Bates system for enhancing visual acuity, analyzed the "money personality," and pioneered a technique for recording dreams. He is presently engaged in a Herculean effort to simultaneously master 200 world languages.

These personal experiments are also mirrored in his work, which demonstrates a keen interest in such salient concepts as hypnotism, telepathy, semantics, "similarization," and Dianetics. These thoughts and others are explored in his numerous books, including such popular works as: *Slan, The World of Null-A, The Voyage of the Space Beagle, The Weapon Shops of Isher, The Winged Man, The Darkness on Diamondia, Children of Tomorrow, Destination: Universe!,* and *Mission to the Stars,* among others.

A. E. van Vogt lives high atop the Hollywood Hills. His home looks warm and lived-in, cluttered with old furniture and memorabilia, most of it collected by his late wife, E. Mayne Hull. Van Vogt is a literary dynamo. He is currently penning several novels and anthologies, as well as mapping out plans for new ventures in film and television. Indeed, he recently completed his first full-length screenplay.

Van Vogt is an impressive man—towering in stature, resolute in tone, ebullient in spirit. He possesses a commanding intellect, a dry wit, and an old-world manner. In many ways, he resembles a fine old watch—delicately tuned, precise in declaration, built with superb workmanship and choice parts.

Van Vogt is the genuine article, a by-product of an earlier day which valued simple virtues and pleasures. There is no condescension in his pitch, haughtiness in his demeanor, falseness in his words, or insincerity in his actions.

Van Vogt's manner is shy, but inviting. His carefully chiselled face highlights his penetrating eyes, robust smile, and demonstrative expressions. This afternoon, he appears healthy, well-rested, and prepared for the discussion which will ensue. As always, van Vogt speaks softly, precisely, eagerly. Flanked by a glass of sherry on one side, and a pile of notes and papers on the other, he proceeds to answer my questions. As I weigh his responses, I am clearly impressed. His answers are striking: comprehensive and without hesitation or embellishment. His voice commands attention. He is both decisive and energetic. He listens to my questions with rapt interest. With skill and polish, he zeroes in on the essential, evidencing a wealth of knowledge and understanding.

JE: What early life experiences inspired your interest in writing?

VV: I've given several answers to this question. But I should report that when I visited my mother in 1961 (when she was age seventy-four), I discovered to my silent astonishment that she took full credit for my being a writer. It seems that when she was carrying me, she read a lot of mystery stories. At the time, she had the thought that she wanted the coming child to be an author of mystery novels. All through my prenatal period she held that thought firmly in her mind. In using the word "silent" a moment ago, I didn't mean to challenge the unscientific nature of her claim. And, in fact, in a world in which people are essentially automatic products of their early conditioning, hers is as good an explanation as any. However, the closest I've come to writing a mystery is *The House That Stood Still*—which has just this year been optioned as a potential movie by an Italian producer-director. My own explanation of why I became a writer is quite different. Actually, I fell out of a second-storey window when I was age two and a half, and was unconscious for three days, near death. Later, using hypnosis, and then still later, Dianetics, in an effort to reduce the trauma of those three days, I discovered that unconsciousness has in it endless hallucinations. The normal part of my brain has probably spent a lifetime trying to rationalize the consequent fantasies and images. This could explain a lot about my bent for science fiction.

JE: Why did you turn to science fiction as a means of expression?

VV: When my family (I was age ten at the time) moved to a small town in Manitoba, Canada, I discovered some books on the teacher's desk. She allowed me to read them, and I often stayed in at recess to do this reading. One of my reasons for staying in during the fifteen minute morning and afternoon play times was, that as a newcomer, I was the same age as the most violent preteeners in the school. Every time I went out, another gang of age nine-ten-eleven year old kids would force me to fight one of their stronger members. I won every such fight; and it was a fair fight—the gang didn't pounce on me in retaliation—but I was a reluctant battler, and felt myself surrounded by hostility. Later, many of these boys became my friends; so it was evidently a normal boyhood situation. One of the books on the teacher's desk was on Napoleon. Several were fairy tales. I read the fairy tales and the book about Napoleon with equal avidity. Unfortunately, the teacher kept urging me to go outside. I had no way to resist her. When she said, "Alfred, you go out and play. It's not a good thing for a boy to read all the time!" . . . I went. But I read my first fairy tales in her classroom. And I discovered that I enjoyed fantasy. My family had a brief interlude move to the city of Winnipeg, Manitoba (1926-1928). It was in Winnipeg in November, 1926, that I saw this strange magazine with the fantastic cover, with the name *Amazing Stories*, on a newsstand. I bought that November issue and subsequent issues. And then in the autumn of 1928, when we were back in Morden, I asked the local druggist to order it for me. He ordered two copies, thinking maybe someone else would be interested. No one else ever bought a copy. The following summer, just before we moved back to Winnipeg, a friend, whose father had a farm, mentioned to me that the farmhands were short of reading material. Did I have anything? I loaned him all my back issues of *Amazing*. Two months later, I asked him to return them. He was surprised. He said, "Oh, they read them, and threw them in the trash. They thought they were a bunch of crazy junk." Actually, this assessment wasn't too far from the truth. With Hugo Gernsback gone, *Amazing* published poorer stories each month. I finally stopped buying it. But I remembered the great stories later on. And I had my background in the field solidly embedded in my mind for the day in 1938 when I picked up the July issue of *Astounding* with the story "Who Goes There?" in it. After reading that remarkable novella, I submitted to John W. Campbell, Jr., the editor, the idea for "Vault of the Beast." When he encouraged me to write it, I was launched.

JE: Are you essentially a self-taught writer?

VV: Yes. I operate in various life situations by what I call "systematic thoughts." In my early years, I read numerous books on writing. I finally found a combination of systems which I learned the way one learns a discipline. I wrote my stories in what the author of my most treasured text on writing called "fictional sentences." The first story I ever sold was a confession-type, which was bought by the *True Story* magazine chain. It was 9,000 words long. And so it probably contains 1,000-1,200 sentences. I consciously—and this is what discipline (system) means—wrote every one of the 1,000 as a fictional sentence. For a confession story, this required that every sentence have an emotion in it. The treasured text, which I just mentioned, was *The Only Two Ways to Write a Story*, by John W. Gallishaw. Gallishaw had observed in the best writers of his day, also, that they wrote stories in what was roughly a series of 800-word scenes. Each scene divided into five steps. And this system I also did in my disciplined way. No piece of music was ever more rigidly organized than the five steps of these scenes—the wordage could vary slightly, but not much. In my naivete at the time, I thought I was revealing one of my precious secrets, when I discussed my method back in 1948, in an article on writing science fiction, which was published in Lloyd Eshbach's *Of Worlds Beyond*. So far as I know, though, only one writer—and I may have misheard him—subsequently told me that he has found the method valuable. In the years that followed, I read a variety of comments on my 800-word scenes. Without exception, everybody had misread the description. An English professor, quoting an American critic, wrote in *Foundation*, an excellent science fiction publication issued quarterly in England, that I changed the entire direction of my story every 800 words, and that no doubt this was the reason I was known as the master of confusion.

JE: Closely related to your 800-word scenes is your use of story "hang-ups." How do they figure into your approach?

VV: Early in my career, a major technique of mine was to write a "hang-up" into every sentence. The reader who tried to skim, as critics tend to do (they just want to get an idea of what the story is about) would quickly bog down, because he wasn't making the contribution to each sentence that the method required. My regular readers don't get confused, because they're able to make the necessary contribution. The hang-up in each sentence was, by my theory, the science fiction "fictional sentence." A science fiction fictional sentence, as I write it, has to have a hang-up in it, ideally. My first science fiction story—though it wasn't the first published—"Vault of the Beast," opened: "The creature crept." The reader doesn't know what kind of creature. That is the hang-up. Another sentence: "This caricature of a human shape reached into one of those skin folds with that twisted hand, and drew out a small, gleaming metal object." There are four hang-ups in that sentence. When I wrote confession-type stories, every sentence, as I mentioned earlier, had to contain an emotion in it. For example, you don't say, "I lived at 323 Brand Street." You say, "Tears came to my eyes as I thought of my tiny bedroom at 323 Brand Street." If your story has 1,000 sentences in it, every sentence should have an emotion in it. It is my belief that stories written with these hang-ups, particularly, will endure longer than other types of stories. The reason is simple: readers of each generation will contribute meaning from their own time, their own era, filling in the gaps with data that I don't have now, or didn't have when I wrote the story.

JE: A number of prominent themes loom large in your work, one of which is the "superman" motif. Are there others of equal importance?

VV: I am told that the "superman" theme permeates my stories. However, that's a superficial view of what I'm up to. Looking back, I have to surmise that I was smarter than I realized. I early saw the problem of the life-death cycle, and wondered if the cycle could be—and this is really the correct word (and thought)—extended. In my stories, accordingly, I explored one immortality option after another. And I would guess that a combination of medical science (for disease), physical exercise, formal psychotherapy, and mental warding-off mechanisms (or philosophies) for avoiding the shock and stress from the grimmer aspects of everyday existence, is the beginning of the answer.

JE: How extensively do you research a novel before sitting down to write it?

VV: When I work on a story, I read extensively about the science—or whatever—necessary for the underlying factual accuracy. And, of course, any major interest gets put into my current stories. In *Pendulum*, for example, I use some unusual dialects—sparingly, of course, but enough to indicate that I've familiarized myself with two little-known languages: Frisian, a dialect of north Holland, and Raeto-Romanic, the fourth language of Switzerland. Many people have heard of this last, but no one else ever—except myself—was interested enough to find out what kind of language it was. (It's another way that ancient Latin came up to modern times.) In writing my Red China novel, *The Violent Man* (not science fiction), starting in 1954, I began to accumulate books on China and Communism, and altogether in the eight years it took me to write this double-length novel, I read and re-read about 100 basic books on the subject. This novel was reissued in 1978 by Pocket Books, a major United States paperback publisher. Among my science fiction, probably my two non-Aristotelian novels, *The World of Null-A* and *The Players of Null-A*, are my most obviously well-researched stories, since they deal with the ideas of Alfred Korzybski as expounded in his masterwork, *Science and Sanity*. These novels have probably interested more people in General Semantics than any other books, science fiction or otherwise.

JE: Do you make a conscious attempt to portray a specific view of science in your work?

VV: I accept science as an attempt to establish an orderly explanation of everything that has happened in the universe since the Big Bang. It has, however, been interesting to observe that at least a couple of generations of scientists got involved (as a consequence of the positive philosophy of the last century) in promoting specific, limited explanations of this or that phenomenon, and that there are still a lot of people around who accept the current theorems as if they were the word of God, instead of, possibly, being intermediate explanations for what may eventually be a more comprehensive understanding of the "reality" of things. If there is any particular view of science in my work, it is most likely that science is, at this intermediate stage, evaluating the dynamic truth of the enigma that underlies all that we perceive in the surrounding continuum.

JE: Given the tremendous emphasis you place on logic, how important is imagination in the context of your writing?

VV: Writing science fiction has been a major cause for the development of both my imagination and my sense of logic. Everything I wrote, or studied in connection with writing, expanded my consciousness. Studies that I made which began as imagination often ended up as systematic thoughts, by which I subsequently handled my life and my associations with other people. There has been a continual feedback between imagination and reality. And I believe this also happens to people who read science fiction.

JE: Do you have a particular "system" when it comes to creating story characters?

VV: Yes. To identify minor characters, I assign them a neuroticism: that's character, by my system. The gooder the good guy, the less character he has, by these standards. So in him, I place a timeless truth. Gosseyn, in the *Null-A* stories, is a General Semantician. When Patricia and he sleep in adjoining twin beds in the same room, she's in no danger. Fully trained General Semantic types don't become sexually involved with neurotic members of the opposite sex. In *Slan*, Jommy is a telepath and a morally superior mutation. In *Voyage of the Space Beagle*, Grosvenor is trained in, and manifests, Nexialism.

JE: In recent years, your approach to writing has come in for some rather harsh criticism. Has your style changed significantly over the years?

VV: It's only in recent years that what used to be called "slick" writing has appeared in science fiction. Is it a permanent change? For years, until the 1960s, I consciously wrote pulp-style sentences. They have a certain lush poetry in them. In the late 1960s, I began to concentrate on content and even allowed my protagonist to be neurotic, also. However, these current stories don't seem to win the same approval as when I followed the earlier system. Will *Future Glitter* and *The Anarchistic Colossus* be reissued as often as *Slan* and the *Null-A* stories? Time will tell.

JE: Can you say something about the genesis of a story? What comes first?

VV: A number of my recent stories are the result of luncheons I had with film or television producers, directors, or story editors. For example, I had lunch with an early story editor of *Outer Limits*, a television science fiction series.

Prior to the luncheon, I had thought of a dramatic opening that might fit into the series. After listening to it, he said, in effect, "If you can work up a satisfactory story to continue from that opening, you've got a sale." Well, I couldn't—in terms of thinking of it as television. But several years later, using that beginning, I wrote the short story, "The Ultra Man," which is part of a collection published in the United States under the title *Worlds of A. E. van Vogt*. That is typical of my trying to fit in with someone else's format. I should have known. On the two or three occasions that John W. Campbell, Jr., the editor of *Astounding*, offered me one of his ideas, he was rewarded by getting the story back three or four years later. Similarly, I started a story for each producer who talked to me. Some of these unfinished items sit in boxes in the garage under my house. I recently finished several of these, and they are included in *Pendulum*, the new collection from DAW. Such a lengthy gestation time has been extremely damaging to my television and film career. Since my 1969 new theory of rapid writing, I am better—meaning faster. For example, George Hay in England has twice gotten stories from me for original anthologies. What he offers is a theme.

JE: To what extent do you know what you're going to write before you put it down on paper?

VV: If the question means, do I have a complete outline before I start writing, the answer is "no." It used to take me two years to write a science fiction novel. During that time, though, I also worked on shorter-length fiction. But the job of reasoning out, and writing, a 70,000 word novel was done piecemeal. In 1969, as I mentioned, I thought of a faster method. After having any kind of thought as to what the story was about, I would write that out first. It was obvious, then, that what I had written would require specific developments. So I wrote those. Sometimes, what I wrote in this piecemeal fashion was only three lines, but it could be as much as three pages. As soon as I had four or five such bits, they logically required either earlier or later developments, which I wrote. Presently, I had a 100 pages or so, usually including parts of the beginning, middle, and ending. So with that much completed, I could begin at the beginning and work out the missing sections. By this means, I discovered I could work on several novels at the same time.

JE: Do you do much rewriting in the course of a book?

VV: My principal rewriting has always been going back and adding ideas that are needed to lead up to story situations that evolved later in the story. I used to, when I had my first draft finished, start at the beginning and change words in order to add certain sounds, according to a theory I had that emotion could be evoked subliminally. (Before I ever heard that word, I called it "ritual emotion.") For some scenes, this meant adding words with the d and t sounds in them, for others the liquid sounds m, n, and l, and g (unvinculated) and j, p and b, v and f, etc. Depending on the emotion I wanted, I sustained each set of sounds as long as that particular situation continued. For example, consider this battle scene: "The line of fire *c*rept along the length of the enemy battleship. The effe*c*t was beyond *C*lane's anticipation. The flame li*c*ked high and bright. The night *c*ame alive with the *c*orus*c*ating fury of that immense fire. The dar*k* land below spar*k*led with refle*c*ted glare." In this passage, I substituted words with the "k" sound in them wherever I could find one with a similar meaning to the one being replaced. I felt this created a subliminal emotional effect on the reader suitable for battle scenes. Now, if you argue that there could be a lot more "k" sounds inserted in such a paragraph, my answer would be that I didn't want a poetic effect, or even simple alliteration, that would be obvious. I've done that, but for different reasons. After my writing style came in for extensive criticism, I thought, "Well, maybe I'm wrong." These days, instead, I merely aim in the general direction of such techniques. Principally, I now concentrate on greater story content.

JE: Is seclusion a necessary requirement in order to write?

VV: What I need is not to have my train of thought interrupted too often. Within that frame, I can do minor chores around the house, go to the store, read the newspaper ten minutes at a time, answer the phone (if it doesn't ring too often). And so I get through my work day, which often lasts from 10 a.m. to 11 p.m.

JE: Do you write with some ideal audience in mind?

VV: Obviously, if *Astounding* hadn't existed in 1938, I wouldn't have written a story for it. But granting that publications are available, and open to freelance submissions, it wasn't the readership I thought about. I was the audience. As a science fiction audience, I reflect intellectuality and a degree of Victorian morality, even though I know the facts of life perhaps better than most, since I conducted psychotherapy experiments from 1951 to 1962, using Dianetic techniques, on nearly 2,000 people.

JE: How important does impact figure in your concerns?

VV: If there is an answer to that question, I suppose it is that I write scared. My feeling is that if I use one sentence too many, will lose my reader. What this means, at times, is that I won't use an entire sentence, but only a portion of one. Some thoughts, or progressions, are so tiny they should have only one word devoted to them. The consequent impact on the reader is of story action that never stops.

JE: Are there books you've written that you wish, in retrospect, were never published?

VV: No. I have no regrets on any of my stories. Science fiction is a form of genre writing. When I discovered that I had a keen interest in science fiction genre, I didn't say, "Damn it, why can't I be interested in a type of writing that will win me artistic respect?" Perhaps, I started with too small an ego. I learned how to do something in a craftsmanlike way. That something was science fiction, which provided feedback and an intellectual growth that was not anticipated by the early practitioners. Automatically, I grew as a person. I didn't have to fight my way up. I floated up. According to my critics, my best stories were written early in my career. My own feeling is that some of my recent books are better. But it's not a problem with me. I'm like the individual who did crossword puzzles in his early days instead of spending the time on something "useful." And then later it turned out (a recently discovered truth) that doing crossword puzzles is one of the ways to a high IQ. Some of my early stories, in spite of all my scheming, have old-fashioned ideas in them. But I know what the scheme was. The story is not responsible for my bad guess as to what the world might be like in the 1970s. Of the three principal genre-type writings—mystery, western and science fiction—science fiction is the only one that can have bad guesses in it. By the way I wrote, requiring the reader to fill in the hang-ups in my sentences, I largely avoided bad predictions.

JE: Do you think that your writing has steadily improved over the years?

VV: About ten years ago, a supervising editor at Doubleday read two of my books, *The Weapon Shops of Isher* and *The Weapon Makers*, with an eye to some kind of special book club publication. He turned them down on the grounds—so I was told—that I had improved greatly in my writing style since turning out those novels. It's interesting to note that the present editor of Pocket Books, when inquiring what of my work was contractually available for paperback publication, asked first about those two novels. Both volumes have since been published by Doubleday and, according to a recent report, are doing extremely well. In terms of writing style, I must put myself on the fence. As a young writer, I was an organized craftsman. I also had some odd beliefs. For example, I considered the 800-word scene a "rhythm" in the story. I also believed that the use of certain letters in excess of the normal, but short of poetic effect, constituted a "rhythm." In executing the twists of language required by my methods did I offend English majors of the 1950s and 1960s, or did I actually abuse the English language? I'm currently in the process of learning 200 languages. When I've mastered them all, I shall be a better judge of such matters.

JE: Does your emotional state affect your ability to write?

VV: I suppose I'm a "square." I don't have emotional states, at least not for long. The squares of this world are the essentially stable people. The emotional types are often more stimulating as individuals. The reasons—by one of my systematic thoughts—is that they somehow had a direct contact opened for them with the subconscious mind. I achieve the creative benefits derived from such contact, with one or more of the dozen thought systems with which I operate. This is not to suggest that I don't sometimes detect stirrings of such emotions as anger, or pleasure, or fear. I do.

JE: Do you consciously file away ideas for future stories?

VV: During the period, 1950-1962, when I was most involved in the study of human behavior, I wrote bits of various stories. How good were those bits? There were portions of all three *Silkie* novelettes (which I eventually organized into a novel). There was the beginning of *The Battle of Forever*, my favorite far-out novel. There were portions of *The Darkness of Diamondia, Future Glitter, Children of Tomorrow,* and *The Secret Galactics*. There were also parts of the three novels on which I've recently been working. And there were portions of several dozen short stories, some of which were finally finished and published in *The Book of van Vogt*, as well as several parts of short stories which appear in *The Worlds of A. E. van Vogt*. I cannot say, however, that these bits and pieces were on "file." I spent many hours searching through boxes for sheets of paper that had on them scrawled versions of various stories. My guess is that there are at least another ten novels in similar form, not to mention twenty to thirty short stories which I haven't located.

JE: You're extremely good at giving your characters interesting names. Do you follow any set rules?

VV: I discussed the origin of the name, "Gosseyn," for example, in the introduction to *The World of Null-A*. I first saw that name, spelled exactly that way, in an English book about the Middle East. "Gosseyn" was a Middle East chieftain who lived approximately 2,000 years ago. It seemed to be an unusual English-sounding name. At the time, I made no attempt to pronounce it. Much later, my agent, Forrest Ackerman, pointed out that it could be pronounced "Go-Sane," which, of course, is what *Null-A* is about. In *Slan*, my main character has a fairly unusual English name: "John Thomas Cross." I called him

"Jommy" at age nine, to get the "boy" effect (even though as a "Slan," he was much above any nine-year-old human). I called him "Jommy Cross" at age fifteen, when mentally he was as developed as a grown man (I hoped to retain a youthful flavor). As an adult "Slan," I called him "Cross," using only his last name. How do you depict someone smarter than a human being? You can use techniques like that.

JE: What degree of reality do your characters have for you after you've finished writing about them?

VV: That's a touchy subject with me. In my opinion, there's a false belief extant that, in some novels, science-fictional or mainstream, there's such a thing as "good" characterization. The author—it's felt by some people—reaches down into the inner being of human beings, and triumphantly pulls out, and shows us, a true-to-life character. This is absolutely impossible in our day and age. We're presently in a middle period of history. Given our elementary knowledge of human psychology, we simply do not have the insights to accomplish that task. In truth, everyone is, or was, an automatic product of un-scientific conditioning and of the casual accidents that occur in an un-knowing environment. In my novel, *The Man With a Thousand Names*, for example, I describe a super-rich man's son who takes full advantage of his father's great wealth. He is basically a neurotic individual and, I suppose, I do a rather skillful job of describing his character. If that's what you mean by characterization, then I've probably created one of my best characters. From my perspective, though, the depiction of someone else's neurosis is not meaningful, even if it may prove interesting to other "automatics." My characters are often people in search of their identity. I believe that's the best anyone can do in our period of history. The protagonist is constantly in search of himself. In *The World of Null-A*, the search arrives at a meaningful—or meaningless point—when a live "Gosseyn" looks down at a dead "Gosseyn." The last line of the novel reads: "The face was his own."

JE: To what extent does your writing reflect your own search for identity?

VV: I early observed that identity was not an identifiable condition. Instead, I had certain situations wherein I, whoever I was, became disturbed. My therapeutic purposes were aimed at eradicating those things that disturbed me, and I have essentially accomplished that purpose.

JE: How much value do you place on what the critics think of your work?

VV: Apparently, we shall have critics with us from now until the far future. Let me say, to begin with, I don't mind fan critics at all. I really don't care if a fan likes or dislikes my work, so long as he has only a limited fan magazine market to peddle his ideas—in fact, I enjoy reading what he has to say. However, when it comes to criticism in the national circulation magazines, alas, I have lived long enough to know that a hostile reviewer can do great damage to an author; and great damage has been done to me. There are essentially two kinds of critics: one represents a "new wave," and he has a yen to let the readership know that anything written prior to the new thought lacks true reality—which is what he represents. Most realities in fiction evolve through an up curve and then a down curve in about ten years, after which, unless the author can make a shift, the new "new wave" flows over him. The other type of critic is a person, often resident in New York, who can't seem to make a living at writing science fiction; but he knows everybody, and they want to do something for him. As is often the case, he is given the critic's column to write. If he would be calm, and accept the manna from heaven for what it is, fine!, but no, he's angry inside—at what, who knows? He quickly forgets that he's a charity case and begins to act like God Almighty. Can anything be done for him? Will this system ever change? No! Editors in New York are really amazingly strong people. Every day they have to resist buying a story from someone who needs the money in order to eat that day. The wonder is that any stories are bought from out-of-towners. But the editor's soft heart is hardened by one simple reality: the publisher's greed does not allow more than an occasional charitable sale to take place. For this reason—the simple truth of capitalist competition—writers everywhere in the country can compete fair and square. But the critics are principally residents in or near New York. Let me say that, when there is an exception (which occasionally does happen), he doesn't last long, because who wants to read all those books month after month? And as a second reason, he sends in a column or two from the hinterland so engagingly written, that the publisher happens to read it before the editor can hide it, so it somehow gets in.

JE: How do you see your image as it currently manifests itself?

VV: I really believe there's room for everybody. I probably have as many readers as I ever had. Some writers—like Ray Bradbury and Isaac Asimov—expanded into reader groups that have shown no inclination to become involved in the science fiction field as such. They have added to their reading, on the one hand, works by scientists—like Isaac Asimov—who write science fiction, and on the other, works by poets—like Ray Bradbury—who also write science fiction. Some new wave writers have expressed detestation of *Perry Rhodan*. It's like attacking *Tom Swift and His Electric Car*. There's no competition for the new wave. If *Perry Rhodan* disappeared, not a single reader would be available to the new wave. Everybody has his own place and his own audience. My stories show a different type of creativity than any of those persons I've named. It so happens that right now the market for what I do isn't in the millions for each new book of mine. Since my science fiction is consciousness-expanding, I expect that one of these days readers will appreciate in larger numbers what I do. Then I, also, shall become rich like Bradbury and Asimov. Until then, things are middling good. I have no complaints.

JE: If you were asked to assess your work, how would you do so?

VV: Over the years, here in the United States, three groups of science fiction writers have enjoyed greater popularity than I. The leading writers of Group One are Robert Heinlein, Arthur Clarke, and Isaac Asimov, all of whom have known scientific training. I believe that there is a growing audience which, in reading science fiction, requires the assurance that what they read is a genuine extrapolation from true science. The rapid rise of Jerry Pournelle, who has several Ph.Ds., is a further evidence of the importance of a scientific background for this particular audience. Group Two is headed by Ray Bradbury, Ursula LeGuin, Roger Zelazny, and Harlan Ellison. These are all persons who write wonderfully condensed fictional sentences—meaning, their use of the English language is unusually pure and beautiful. All of these writers accept human nature at its present level without argument, and seem to believe that is all there is, ever. And so the vast audience of television and film is within the reach of what they write about. And they have penetrated the fabulous women's market. I suspect that Ellison will eventually have to remove the four-letter words from future revisions of his works, because pornographic language always runs in cycles. I seem to detect that interest in the current cycle is waning. Group Three is headed by Robert Silverberg. He has an extreme ability for finding touching themes, as in *Dying Inside*. His are not sentimental stories. They have genuine feeling in them. There are also a few special individuals, like Frank Herbert, of whose education I know nothing. And then there is my own favorite, R. A. Lafferty. I don't know what his audience is. What I have isn't merely extrapolation of science. I've devised actual practial sub-branches of economics, psychology, education, physical fitness, politics, libertarianism, criminology, etc. None of this will displace, or transcend, the science fiction poets, the scientists-writers, or the marvelously sensitive women writers who have entered the science fiction writing field. But I believe what I have done will eventually exert an influence on modern thought.

JE: Is science fiction writing as challenging today as it was when you began your career?

VV: The science fiction field is in a confused state. The number of paperback science fiction books on the newsstands is awesome. However, we have to remember that in the United States there are over 200 million people, and most of them are over nine years old—which is the age that science fiction reading begins for many. Until evidence of disaster emerges I shall merely continue about my business of writing whatever interests me. At present, most of that writing is science fiction. I still do it as a craftsman. And so there's no special challenge for me that's different from the past. I know my business.

JE: Finally, do you still enjoy reading science fiction? If so, whose work do you admire?

VV: I read the first few paragraphs of every story in all the science fiction magazines published in English. If those paragraphs have story energy in them, I may read on. And if that holds me, then I will read the story. I also receive all the Doubleday book club selections. With them, I also read the first few paragraphs. In addition, I buy several paperbacks a month, and get others free, and do the same with them. My general impression: there's less action in stories these days, but some very ingenious ideas. Of the non-action writers, R. A. Lafferty writes (for me) the best fictional sentences, Robert Silverberg the best true emotion, Harlan Ellison the most condensed fictional sentences, Larry Niven the best hardcore science fiction, Randall Garrett the best pastiche writing, and Jerry Pournelle the farthest in the shortest time. Of the great ladies, C. J. Cherryh, Vonda McIntyre, Katherine Kurtz, Marion Zimmer Bradley, Alice Sheldon (James Tiptree, Jr.), Chelsea Quinn Yarbro, and Tanith Lee have all gone up into those rarefied heights that only women can attain. But the fact that I have to list that many names, and omit several dozen that have my respect—for example, John Brunner and Brian Aldiss—tells me that the field has changed drastically for the better.

POUL ANDERSON:

Seer of Far-Distant Futures

Thoughtful, sensitive, introspective—that is Poul Anderson—one of the "giants" of the science fiction world. No brief introduction can possibly do justice to this seasoned writer, a man whose work stands as a proud monument to his craftsmanship and artistry. An eclectic talent, Anderson has fashioned hundreds of stories of high adventure, space opera, and hard science, all with skill and finesse.

Prior to this interview, I sought out various science fiction writers who knew Anderson and his work. In addition, I tracked down a number of Anderson enthusiasts, readers who devour his books with relish and delight. To a person, they praised his talent and spoke lovingly of his contributions to the field. Unwilling to rest on his laurels, Anderson has continually set a higher and higher standard for himself. His work has steadily improved with age, and his interests have mushroomed to keep pace with his inquisitiveness. Despite his acknowledged popularity, Anderson has eschewed the lure of formula fiction. Instead, he has experimented with new genres, with new stylistic devices, in a constant effort to improve his prose and broaden his perspective on the universe.

In meeting Poul Anderson, I half-expected to meet a man who took his reputation for granted, who might be affected by his celebrity status. Nothing could be less true. A renowned talent, Anderson gives little vent to the idiosyncracies of fame. There is none of the brashness, arrogance, or conceit that might come with the turf. Indeed, he is a man of disarming simplicity, quiet modesty, and reasoned wisdom that comes from having survived the vicissitudes of the field to become one of the most respected names in science fiction.

Poul Anderson is an unpretentious man. Clearly, no one would take him on first meeting, for a famous writer. One cannot help but feel awed, however, by the proportions of the man—not his physical size, but the size of his talent and humanity. Anderson is generous, gracious, giving. He genuinely desires to be helpful. There is no falseness in his manner. His tone is authoritative, confident, the tone of one who is sure of his opinions and secure in his person. His sentences are weighed and measured; no unintentional words exit his lips. His politeness and the cordial way he responds are shorn of excess. His demeanor is courteous, restrained, his smile warm and sincere. Despite his assurance, one is immediately struck by his modesty, his shyness. His voice is soft, somewhat inaudible. His approach is subdued, rather low-keyed.

Anderson's responses today are erudite and precise, reflecting a keen desire to be understood. He speaks much the way a college professor might—with academic reserve, intellectual honesty, and personal objectivity. Anderson is clearly aware of his strengths as well as his weaknesses, and he is willing to discuss both with equal candor, albeit some modesty. No attempt is made to conceal, to beguile, to impress.

While having lunch at a local bistro, on a rainy Los Angeles day, I start to think about the man and the many books which bear his name, classic works, such as *Trader to the Stars, A Midsummer Tempest, Fire Time, The Winter of the World, Tau Zero, The Rebel Worlds, Beyond the Beyond, The Byworlder, The Star Fox, War of the Wing-Men,* and so many others. As Anderson downs his lunch—a huge hamburger, a crisp salad, and a schooner of beer—I ready myself for the conversation which ensues.

JE: Why did you become a writer?

PA: In my case, it was something I drifted into. My ambition was to be a physicist. In fact, I took a degree in physics. Throughout my college years, I wrote a variety of things, mainly as a hobby. Then I graduated into a recession when jobs were hard to get. I thought I would try to support myself through writing while I looked around for work. Somehow, that *while* got longer and longer, and it eventually dawned on me that writing was what I really wanted to do.

JE: How did you find your way into science fiction?

PA: I've been an avid reader of it ever since childhood. As a young boy, I wrote a good deal of science fiction, but it wasn't worth much. I never gave thought to submitting it anywhere. Eventually, though, I came to the conclusion that it was good enough to send, and it was indeed accepted.

JE: Did you start out with the idea of writing science fiction on a full-time basis?

PA: Not really. There wasn't any particular moment of conscious decision on my part. I never intended to write science fiction exclusively and, in fact, I've written a variety of other things. There's no question, though, that science fiction has comprised the largest part of what I've done.

JE: Did you ever worry at the outset, given the period in which you began, that you might not be able to support yourself by writing science fiction?

PA: As a matter of fact, I was faced with that situation on several occasions. Fortunately, I got other jobs that carried me over until things improved. As a young fellow, I had a variety of jobs. Once I worked in a shop that produced giant rabbits for floats. The longest such period, I suppose, was nine or ten months. That was more than twenty years ago.

JE: What was it about science fiction that intrigued you to the extent of wanting to make it your specialty?

PA: Oh, I suppose there were several things that interested me. I was entranced by the general wonder of science itself. I was excited by the way science fiction brought into focus the marvels of the universe in human terms. It was and is one of the few remaining enclaves of old-fashioned story-telling.

JE: Did you have any formal training as a writer?

PA: None whatsoever.

JE: Did that ever pose a problem?

PA: I might or might not have done better initially had I had more training.

It's hard to tell. There's a saying that's probably true of me, although, doubtless, not true of every writer—namely, that you have to write a million words of unsalable copy before you learn enough to write something that someone might buy. I suppose I approximated that number of words. As I think about it, though, I doubt that formal training would have helped, and, I suppose, it might actually have hurt. I've seen quite a number of very promising talents stifled by majoring in creative composition. They got buried under a weight of theory that they weren't yet ready to handle. I dare say, however, that a few well-chosen courses in English and literature would have helped me a good deal, especially at the outset of my career.

JE: How did your background prepare you to write science fiction?

PA: My background in the sciences has proven extremely helpful. I'm one of the comparatively few people in the field who writes what is called "hard" science fiction, although that is, of course, not the only sort of thing I do. A knowledge of science has given me a great deal to write about. Of course, this need not be true, and is not true, of everybody else who has a background in the sciences.

JE: How would you distinguish "hard" science fiction, especially as you write it, from what might be called "soft" science fiction?

PA: The term itself, "hard" science fiction, originated with the late James Blish, who, afterwards, remarked that his original intention had been greatly misinterpreted. Nowadays, what's usually meant by the phrase is writing which is more or less based on "real" science, actual physics, chemistry, biology, and astronomy, and to a considerable extent extrapolates from this, with a minimum of imaginary laws of nature. An excellent example would be Hal Clement's brilliant novel, *Mission of Gravity*, which is a wonderful travelogue through an imaginary planet. In that book, he constructed a new world, while staying within the limits of what he could calculate, what was physically possible. The only assumption he allowed himself which deviated from known science, was faster-than-light travel, and that was mainly for the purpose of getting his characters onto the scene. At the other extreme would be Ray Bradbury's classic work, *The Martian Chronicles*, in which the Mars he describes is contradicted by virtually everything we know about the planet. However, he didn't let that bother him in writing the novel. I might say, too, that there's nothing wrong with that approach. Whether a work is "hard" or "soft" has nothing whatsoever to do with its literary merit *per se*.

JE: When you started your career, were there people in the science fiction field who gave you much help and encouragement?

PA: In the beginning, I didn't know anyone of "great" stature. I was influenced by other writers, but they never really helped me. I pretty much made it on my own. Eventually, though, like so many other science fiction writers of that period, I received a great deal of help from John W. Campbell, Jr., who was the editor of *Astounding*, or *Analog* as it is known today. He was an absolute fountainhead of brilliant story ideas, which he would give away with both hands to anybody who might want to make a story out of them. Usually, when he bought a story, it would be without comment, although if some point interested him, he might write a lengthy letter about that specific point. On the other hand, when he rejected a story, he would often send a detailed letter indicating why he found it unacceptable. Later on, Anthony Boucher, of *Fantasy & Science Fiction*, was also helpful to me, but not so much in terms of representing a "father image." He had little to say in the way of comments or suggestions, but he was masterful at creating a market for different kinds of stories from those which interested Campbell. He was much more concerned with language than Campbell was, and thus encouraged me to experiment with various literary styles.

JE: Who were your early "heroes" in the science fiction field?

PA: Oh, they were the "greats" who most people list—writers like John W. Campbell, Jr., Robert Heinlein, Clifford Simak, A. E. van Vogt, Isaac Asimov, and Theodore Sturgeon, among others.

JE: Is there a prominent theme or concept which underlies your work?

PA: I don't really know. I don't confine myself to a specific area or approach. I try to be as varied as possible, and not to say the same things over and over again. It would be boring for me as well as my readers. However, there is a basic attitude, I suppose, which underlies my writing—namely, that this is a wonderful universe in which to live, that it's great to be alive, and that all it takes is the willingness to give ourselves a chance to experience what life has to offer. If I preach at all, it's probably in the direction of individual liberty, which is a theme that looms large in my work.

JE: Do you see your work as having a didactic function? Do you endeavor to teach as well as entertain the reader?

PA: Yes, but only in a limited way, and only on specific occasions. After all, the reader isn't interested in a bunch of sermons. If he wants that, he can attend church. My main job is to entertain him, to hold his interest as best I can. I do this, primarily, by keeping the story moving. Since most stories have a basic content, though, I suppose they're bound to reflect certain philosophical overtones. And so, where I can, I try to say something that I feel is important, such as the need for additional scientific research and development. Let's hope that I plant a seed here and there.

JE: In writing science fiction, do you feel the need for final answers in science?

PA: No. I doubt that there are any "final" answers in science, and I certainly don't feel any emotional need for them. There will always be unanswerable questions. The field is, by definition, inexhaustible.

JE: How concerned are you that your work mirror known scientific fact?

PA: Oh, as much as the story requires. That doesn't mean, however, losing respect for the facts. For example, in writing science fiction, I often find it necessary for a spacecraft to travel faster than the speed of light. I try to indicate, though, that this is not because I'm trying to ignore the laws of physics, but that we just don't have all the facts today. There are occasions, however, when I'll write an out-and-out fantasy, which makes no attempt to be scientific. Even there, though, I want it to make sense.

JE: How does a story take shape in your mind? How does it develop?

PA: It depends, really, on the type of story. In a short story, normally, only a limited amount of background and characterization are required, primarily because of a lack of space. In writing a story, though, it's important that the writer know much more about his own universe than the reader ever could. Writing a novel is a complicated task. Once I determine, in a general sense, what I'm going to do, I'll sit down and start planning it in great detail. I'll try to figure everything out I possibly can about the world I'm trying to build. After I've calculated the mathematic skeleton of the story, I'll work on several more arbitrary things, such as drawing maps, identifying place names, researching life on the planet. I'll usually end up with pages and pages of closely written notes, just on that one planet, getting down to elaborate descriptions of flora and fauna. Then I'll start developing individual characters. Here, I'll try to get to the place where the characters can walk through my head without my feeling that I'm pulling the strings. This process helps me to determine the storyline. Along about here, I'll try to sketch the plot, in a general way, not getting too specific, though. I want the characters themselves to govern much of what takes place in terms of the actual story.

JE: To what extent does the story surprise you as it unfolds?

PA: In detail, quite a lot. I can count on at least one surprise per chapter. In general, not too much. I know where the story is headed. But in terms of how it's going to get there, I'm often surprised by what happens.

JE: How meticulous are you when it comes to the actual process of writing?

PA: Very. I'm one of those writers who tends to sweat over each word. On a good day, I might get 2,000 to 3,000 words of first draft, which means working from breakfast to dinner, with no break for lunch. I spend the evening going over it with great care, trying to get the language just right. This continues until my first draft is polished to my liking. I'll then let it cool for awhile. Later, I'll come back, look it over once or twice, and then type up the clean copy. That part goes pretty fast, primarily because so much work has been done already. Even then, however, I'll go over it with a fine toothed comb.

JE: Do you follow a set routine when you're working on a book?

PA As I said, I'll usually work from breakfast to dinner. During that time, I keep the door closed; in fact, I get pretty unpleasant if anyone interrupts me. When I'm working, I take the process quite seriously.

JE: When you write, do you have a particular reader in mind?

PA: Yes and no. Even in the field of science fiction, where there's a high degree of contact between the writer and his readers, the percentage that you ever meet or hear from is very small. A writer doesn't make his money off science fiction fans, but off that anonymous guy he never hears of who buys a book off the shelf. I always try to keep this in mind when I'm writing a book. On the other hand, I value the feedback I get from science fiction fans. They're a great source of encouragement. While I'm working on a book, I'll often say to myself, "so-and-so ought to like this," with a particular individual in mind. But I don't write for any one person.

JE: Do you see yourself as "driven" to write, or do you write primarily in order to make a living?

PA: As a writer, I try to do the very best job I can. However, I write as little as possible, because there are so many other things in life that I enjoy doing. If somebody gave me a million tax-free dollars, I would probably never write again, at least professionally.

JE: Are you concerned with what the critics think about your work?

PA: No. I don't write for the critics; I write for those who buy my books.

JE: Do you feel that the critics tend to understand your work?

PA: On the whole, very little, with, perhaps, a few exceptions. I know a few critics who see what I'm trying to get at. Their rarity doesn't really bother me, though, because there's a substantial number of readers who do.

JE: What accounts for this lack of understanding on the part of the critics?

PA: That's difficult to answer. I don't want my comments to sound like sour grapes. Not even Shakespeare speaks everybody's language. You certainly can't expect the rest of us lesser writers to be universally appreciated, even among readers of taste and discrimination. That's something which very few critics seem to understand. They see themselves as qualified to judge the whole body of literature. In the end, though, I suppose that the motifs and emphases I treat don't appeal to the personality types who work as literary critics.

JE: Are you a harsh critic of your own work?

PA: I try to be. I try to do the best I can. I try to live up to my obligations as a writer. That's the most I can do.

JE: How would you assess your own writing?

PA: The late writer and editor, Anthony Boucher, always used to say that the person least qualified to judge a work is the author himself. In that sense, I agree with him. Really, only time will tell. These days, though, I mostly accomplish what I set out to do. I don't do it perfectly, but I do it so that I'm generally satisfied with the finished product.

JE: Do you strive to have a particular impact on your readers?

PA: Basically, when I write fiction, I'm engaged in the business of telling stories. It's up to me to entertain the reader. After all, my readers give me much more than simply money. That's the smallest part, even though that's what pays the bills. More importantly, they give me time, which is really the only treasure human beings have when you come right down to it. I have to deserve this somehow. I have to give them as much as they give me. My primary business, first, is to entertain them. Now, this doesn't mean my work has to be devoid of thought. In fact, it's this thought, I believe, which helps to explain the tremendous appeal of science fiction. I like to imagine I've given my readers something to think about, especially my young readers. If I'm lucky, I've given then some new way of seeing the world.

JE: What do you think explains your enormous staying power as a writer?

PA: I don't know. Of course, I should mention that others are at least equal in this respect, or more popular. I'm by no means unique; there's Robert Heinlein, Clifford Simak, Isaac Asimov, and many others. It doesn't surprise me, however, that I've managed to keep going this long. What does surprise me is why so many talented writers fail to make it. I just don't know.

JE: To what extent do you expect the reader to understand the numerous scientific references which you make in your work?

PA: That depends entirely on the reader. I try to write in such a way that anybody can follow the story whether or not he understands the scientific references, but that those who do understand them will enjoy it even more. Although we like to think nowadays that everybody understands at least the nuts-and-bolts of science, we know that that's certainly not true. Sadly, most people don't have any idea of what science is all about, including its role in the scheme of things.

JE: Humor seems to play a prominent role in many of your stories. How central is it in your view of writing?

PA: It's very important. In fact, I've written several stories that were nothing more than comedy. Humor not only provides for relief, but is, after all, a significant aspect of human personality. In that sense, it's vital in most works of literature.

JE: You're known as a master of "puzzle" stories. What is the secret of a good puzzle story?

PA: I suppose it goes back to the basic format inherent in the old-fashioned mystery story, of which, incidentally, I've written a fair number. The idea is to set up the problem early on, plant a substantial number of good clues, and then let the reader have the fun of guessing the solution.

JE: Many of your books evidence a deep interest in politics. Is this a conscious objective on your part?

PA: Politics is an inherently fascinating thing in itself. It's also an integral part of life. One way or another, it's bound to show up in science fiction, particularly when you're dealing with alien societies. In the process of inventing new worlds, it's impossible not to touch on politics.

JE: In several of your books, you espouse, either directly or indirectly, the virtues of unrestricted free enterprise. Why do you see capitalism as the most viable economic system?

PA: For two reasons: First, it places the greatest emphasis on individual liberty, thereby permitting individuals to reap the rewards of their own labor, and, second, in a material sense, it's the most productive system anyone has yet evolved.

JE: One of your best known stories is "Sam Hall," a story which deals with personal unrest and rebellion, the battleground being big government. Why has this story evoked such a tremendous response?

PA: Most of the people who read science fiction tend to be individualists in one way or another. They have individualistic personalities, even though they might describe themselves as "liberals" or "conservatives." They tend to be very self-directed people; people who desire to determine the direction of their own lives. I think they identify with independent characters, such as Sam Hall, who struggles to shape his own life, regardless of social pressures.

JE: You are widely heralded as a builder of civilizations. Why did you choose the future history mode in which to work?

PA: It just sort of happened. Of course, I was influenced by Robert Heinlein, who wrote an outstanding future history. As far as I know, the future history approach originated with him. He's a superb writer, as well as a wonderful human being.

JE: How do you go about minimizing the turbulence and unpredictability inherent in writing future histories?

PA: It's largely a matter of keeping extensive notes. I have the time scheme worked out almost year-by-year, although there are some parts I haven't yet developed. I keep elaborate notes on individuals, places, and events as they appear. Everything is carefully filed so that I can use it when I'm writing a new story. I try to review these notes to make sure that everything is consistent.

JE: Your book, *War of the Wing-Men*, represents a skillful attempt to construct an entire alien planet, from physics to biology. Indeed, it was one of the first tales in your future history. How did that book originate?

PA: Oh, that was a long time ago. It has recently been reissued under its proper title, *The Man Who Counts*. It was my first real attempt at world-building, the sort of thing that Hal Clement does so well. Here, I was interested in meeting the challenge, posed years earlier by L. Sprague de Camp, who said that he, for one, could not believe in intelligent beings who flew like birds, because muscle power couldn't raise a big enough body to hold the size of brain that would be required for intelligence. In terms of the book, I designed the planet with a very dense atmosphere. It was a very unearth-like planet. However, I sought to invent a universe in which this was possible.

JE: In that book, you penned Nicholas van Rijn, a powerful and remembered character in science fiction. How would you describe him?

PA: Basically, he's modeled after certain historical types. I might say, however, that I never write a real person into a story, even with a change of names. Naturally, in creating characters, a writer will draw on his experiences with people in general, as well as with people he's encountered in history and literature. Essentially, van Rijn is a composite of several actual figures who were common in the Age of Discovery—the Renaissance and the Reformation. Physically, he's modeled after King Christian IV of Denmark, who was quite a character. I also drew on Falstaff, Long John Silver, and so on. They all came together in the person of van Rijn.

JE: What about the character of van Rijn appeals to you?

PA: He's a real bastard, of course. And yet, he has a certain rascally charm. Also, there's the fact that he's a "Superman" figure, but not in the conventional sense. He's old, fat, ugly, gruff. Somehow, that tickles me.

JE: Several of your books draw extensively on history as well as science. How importantly does history figure as a basis for your story ideas?

PA: It's very important. My whole future history series, which comprises a substantial percentage of my work, draws extensively on the past. I've used history in many of my stories. I don't see how anyone can make sense of the present, let alone construct an imaginary future that makes sense, without having some knowledge of the past.

JE: Some critics contend that your portrayal of women, as expressed in books such as *Trader to the Stars*, reveals a blatantly chauvinistic attitude. Would you concur with that charge?

PA: It's conceivable that they're right, although I certainly never intended to cast women in that light. Over the years, however, I've learned to handle characterization better, especially women characters. For a male writer, it's always more difficult to fashion female characters than it is members of his own sex. In earlier years, I tended to use comparatively few women characters, and usually not to give them leading roles in my stories. That grew out of my fear that I couldn't make them sufficiently plausible. I would like to point out, however, that in this same period, and, even earlier, I published a novel entitled, *Virgin Planet*, in which women were cast in almost heroic terms. In that book, a shipwreck took place. For many years, the planet was inhabited by nothing but women, who reproduced themselves by artificial means, such as cloning. They viewed men as almost god-like figures until, one day, a spaceman happened to land there. It was the archetypal sexual fantasy, except that the book is all about how this poor silly ass blunders from one situation to the next, always having to be rescued by one or another of the women. In spite of all these seeming opportunities, he never quite manages to make out. The book was intended mainly as a comedy, but I think you could call it an antisexist work.

JE: Does a character, such as Jill Conway in *Fire Time*, represent a new attitude toward female characters on your part?

PA: Yes. These days, I feel somewhat more comfortable with female characters. It's interesting, but some women have told me that my female characters tend to be so self-confident in recent works that it gives them an inferiority complex. For example, *The Dancer from Atlantis* is a novel about the kind of women I've met in recent years—strong, independent, proud. In that book, the leading character is absolutely indomitable, regardless of the situations which confront her. *The Winter of the World* depicts a society in which women assume positions of leadership and responsibility. I recently completed a novel, entitled *The Avatar*, in which two or three of the leading characters are women. In fact, one of the women is described as one of the leading intellects of her age.

JE: Your writing is clearly distinguished by its emphasis on detailed explanation. What is your feeling about the need for such explanation? How much is actually required?

PA: That depends a great deal on the individual story, as well as the reader. In my case, I admit it's sometimes a failing. My characters do, at times, tend to deliver lectures. On the other hand, it's a good way for me to convey a lot of information as background for what's going to happen later. I try to be brief, but I recognize that my descriptions sometimes get bogged down in too much detail.

JE: The novel, *The Trouble Twisters*, is a testimonial to your skill at character development. Is it difficult to pen believable charcters in science fiction, especially where so many of the character types are imaginary figures?

PA: I don't think so. After all, people are people. I suspect they'll behave pretty much the same in the future as they have in the past. There's no real difference in constructing a science fiction character as opposed to a here-and-now character.

JE: Science fiction has changed a great deal in recent years. Where do you see the genre going in the future?

PA: I don't see it going toward any one place. I like to quote A. J. Budrys, who's one of our best science fiction writers. He once remarked, "Trends are for second-raters." I think he's right. As I see it, science fiction, ever since the Golden Age, when John W. Campbell, Jr. first took over *Astounding*, has never gone in any one direction. It's gone in all directions, which, I think, is a very good thing. In fact, the dull periods in science fiction have occurred when writers became obsessed with a single motif. At present, we have many fine writers, each one working in a different way. I like that fact. Indeed, more and more, science fiction, as a body of literature, is ceasing to exist. I would like to see the label eliminated altogether. In terms of literary technique, it's becoming more and more like mainstream writing, while mainstream writing is adopting more and more science fiction idiom.

JE: Do you still enjoy writing science fiction today as much as you did when you began your career?

PA: That's asking me to think back a long way. Basically, when I started out, I was primarily concerned with making a living. I wrote very fast, without too much regard for the literary refinements. Over the years, I've shifted more and more the other way, making a conscious effort to develop a polished literary style. I'm more concerned today with characterization, with trying to get the language right, and so on. I suppose I read less science fiction today than before. But that's mainly for lack of time. Now, my wife helps to steer me on to what's good. I'm still enthusiastic, but my emphasis has shifted.

JE: Do you ever feel a sense of competition with other science fiction writers?

PA: No. By and large, it's a very friendly field. My feeling is that a good writer benefits all of us, in the sense that he reflects favorably on the entire field. Moreover, he helps us to think about things in new ways, which is all to the good. The more good writers, the better.

JE: Are you ever bothered by the isolation, the loneliness, which is such an integral part of being a writer?

PA: No, not really. In many ways, writing is a compensation for loneliness. It certainly was when I was in my teens. Besides being stuck out on a farm, I was a very asocial kid, as many writers were. Subsequently, though, I've developed many close friendships and, if anything, my wife and I have more of a social life today than we can readily handle. As for writing itself, I don't feel any sense of loneliness when I'm writing. In fact, I hate it when somebody opens that study door. There's also a camaraderie among science fiction writers and readers. We meet at conventions, we talk to each other, we form close relationships. Sometimes, marriages even result from such meetings, which is how I met my wife. If there's any problem at all, it's how to keep from getting too involved in the social side of it to find time to think, to read, to write.

JE: In a recent interview, Ray Bradbury observed that we've moved into a new period, in which science fiction may well become the literature of the future, owing to the tremendous impact of *Star Wars, Close Encounters*, and other such films. Do you see that happening in the near future?

PA: No. I certainly don't agree with Mr. Bradbury that science fiction is going to become *the* literature of tomorrow. If anything, it seems much more likely that literature as a whole will simply absorb science fiction, something which has already started to happen. In fact, many mainstream writers, such as John Hersey, are employing science fiction idiom more and more in their work. That's because it's now common currency. It's no longer something which only a few nuts are muttering to each other. After all, we're living in an age in which science fiction terms are accepted more or less as natural idiom. On the other hand, I think that many people will still want literature that deals with ideas and concerns which are more immediate and familiar than those commonly treated in science fiction. As for the social effects of science fiction, I certainly don't think it can save the world. I do think, though, that it can do some things which are positive. For one, it's helping to keep literacy alive in this country, which, these days, is no mean feat. In addition, at a time when some people are ranting about the dangers of technology, science fiction continues to be a voice of reason. Finally, there's no doubt that science fiction plays an important part in recruiting scientists and technologists from amongst the young. In this regard, I've known a good many engineers and scientists who readily admit that science fiction is what first hooked them on the sciences, and helped them to get through all those difficult years of hard work and study that one has to go through. In all these cases, science fiction is a vital and positive force for good.

JE: Finally, what do you enjoy doing when you're not writing?

PA: Oh, I have lots of hobbies—reading, gardening, traveling, hiking, sailing, conversing, listening to music, and many other things. There's really no limit to the things that are fun to do. There are also many semi-professional things I enjoy doing—writing letters, translating, and poetry.

ROBERT SILVERBERG:

Next Stop — *Lord Valentine's Castle*

After a four-year hiatus, Robert Silverberg has returned to science fiction writing, the proud recipient of the highest advance ever paid a science fiction author for a single book. Silverberg's new novel, *Lord Valentine's Castle*, garnered a hardcover bid of $127,500 by Harper & Row, coupled with 15 percent royalties and a guaranteed advertising budget of $35,000.

The book itself promises to excite not only science fiction enthusiasts, but mainstream readers as well. Indeed, Silverberg views this novel as possibly his biggest book to date, reaching a wide spectrum of the American reading public. According to the author, *Lord Valentine's Castle* will be a long epic adventure set on an extra-solar planet approximately 20,000 years from now. It is estimated that the book will run anywhere from 150,000 to 200,000 words and be completed by June, 1979.

A titan in the science fiction field, Robert Silverberg has come out of retirement to tell, he hopes, that big story which has eluded him so far. Although he boasts a legion of important and successful books, he has yet to write that major work which will bring together readers of all genres for a common science fiction experience. This novel promises such results, which is why publishers clamored at his door when word leaked out about *Lord Valentine's Castle*. During his four-year layoff, Silverberg was courted by numerous publishers who sought to tie him down to one project or another. He steadfastly turned down all offers, determined not to write again. And then, much to his amazement, a story idea came to him—one which he could not turn down. It came from within and it took shape in an eighteen-page outline, which became the basis of *Lord Valentine's Castle*.

There are few writers in the science fiction field who possess the unique talents of Robert Silverberg, a genuine literary craftsman, whose fiction embodies those special qualities which typify his writing, and enabled him to produce such memorable works as *Tower of Glass, Downward to the Earth, Son of Man, Dying Inside, The Book of Skulls, To Live Again, Hawksbill Station, Nightwings, A Time of Changes*, and a myriad of other books and short stories. Few science fiction readers have not been enriched and inspired by his contributions to the genre, contributions which reflect his love of the field and his deep respect for its readers.

Although Silverberg is still writing *Lord Valentine's Castle*, there is every reason to expect it to measure up to or surpass his previous novels. As Thomas Clareson states, "He (Silverberg) will tell a good story, he will fuse together content and form, and he will add to our perception of the human condition. I am certain of these things for only one reason. Robert Silverberg is the complete writer."

The interview below takes place at Silverberg's handsome ranch-style home in Oakland, California, high above the city. Here, we discuss his return to writing—at least *Lord Valentine's Castle*—and why he was wrong when he said that commercial science fiction was no place for a serious writer. Moreover, he describes his own development, both as a writer and a human being, and how the four-year layoff contributed to his growth and maturation.

JE: Can you say something about why you went into retirement in 1974?

RS: Certainly. I had been writing on a full-time basis for almost twenty years at that point and, of course, writing very prolifically. I was very tired. The words were swimming on the page, no longer making much sense to me. However, when I did retire, the element of fatigue was not uppermost in my mind. In 1974, as you know, the nation was experiencing an economic recession, coupled with the systemic consequences of Watergate. That situation bore on me personally, in the sense that all of my books disappeared from print, precisely at the time I needed the emotional support of having those books stay on the shelves. When I approached the publishers, who were having their own economic problems, they showed very little interest in reissuing the books. At the same time, they indicated a great deal of interest in books that I regarded as trivial by comparison. So it was very easy for me to say, with a sulky plague-on-all-your-houses attitude, the hell with it. I'm going to tend my garden and never write again. Well, it was a premature kind of sulk, because very shortly my books began coming back into print as part of the normal publishing cycle, and now, wherever you look, you will see dozens of Silverberg novels. In my weariness, I had simply misread a short-term phenomenon for a permanent trend. However, the element of fatigue was certainly a major factor in my decision. I haven't written now for almost four years. I feel very well rested, thank you. I needed, evidently, a long period in which to recharge my batteries. I merely found various superficial pretexts to justify the fact that I was really weary of sitting at the typewriter and making up galactic epics.

JE: Did you envision your retirement, then, as a permanent thing, or did you view it more as a simple respite?

RS: I certainly intended it as permanent. In fact, until I decided to break my retirement, just a few months ago, it was still permanent. There is an additional problem that I had to work through. The books that I had been writing in the last few years before I quit were becoming increasingly literary in tone, increasingly challenging to write, increasingly difficult to read. I had been getting more and more away from the notion of science fiction as story-telling, and I had begun to think of myself as a sort of James Joyce or Marcel Proust. That was a good thing for a writer to do; to stretch his reach as much as possible. But I found that I was stretching myself beyond the capacity of most of the audience; that I was heading right down a dead-end, as happened to Messrs. Joyce and Proust, where I couldn't carry the theory of what I was doing any further. I wrote myself right into silence with those books. As a result, it was impossible for me to think of writing again until I was able to come to grips with this problem. By the time I was ready to approach a publisher with a book again, it was with a book that was quite different in concept from the *Dying Inside, The Book of Skulls*, and *Born with the Dead* kind of thing I was writing in the early 1970s.

JE: Did you give much thought, at the time you made your decision, as to how you might spend your retirement?

RS: Yes, indeed. I've always been interested in plants, particularly in exotic, strange science fiction plants. Here in California, with this wonderful climate, I wanted to experiment to see what kinds of alien plants I could grow. Actually, I had been doing that all along. But now, having eliminated the distraction of having to write books, I could devote myself to it much more fully. Also, there were a lot of things I wanted to read, things I wanted to learn about myself, places I wanted to visit. It seemed to me at the point when I quit, in 1974, that writing was simply getting in the way of what I really wanted to do. When a writer reaches that point, the wisest thing for him to do is stop writing. I've gone through that phase, which is why I'm about to write a new book.

JE: As you assess that period, in what ways did your retirement contribute to your own maturation, both as a writer and a human being?

RS: At the time I quit writing, I voluntarily abandoned a very successful career, despite the fact that many of my books were out of print. I had won all sorts of awards and publishers were still courting me for new novels. To be able to walk away from all that and say, "I don't want this, I don't need this," gave me a great rush of strength and security. The notion that I didn't need to be Robert Silverberg, world-famous science fiction writer, to support my own identity, but that I could just shrug and play with my cacti and be myself, was an interesting and important thing to discover about myself. In addition, this period gave me the opportunity to get out and interact with people. Writing is a very solitary business. You sit at your desk and type. And you're all alone while you're doing it. It consumes an enormous amount of energy. I'm basically a pretty solitary man to begin with, and when I'm embarked on a major project, I get three times as solitary. So with not writing, I was able to get out and be with people in a way that I hadn't managed since my adolescence. I started writing, of course, when I was still in college. I had those twenty years of full-time, very active writing, at the end of which I was still a relatively young man. That's one thing, incidentally, that pleases and surprises me. People who have been reading me since they were in the seventh grade, finally meet me and discover that I'm not sixty-four years old, and they say, "Oh, I thought you would be a much older man." This gets increasingly pleasing to hear.

JE: How has your attitude toward writing changed, if any, as a result of your self-imposed layoff?

RS: I've gone through a number of changes in my attitude toward writing since I first began nearly twenty-five years ago. At first, it was just a job. I was a bright kid, right out of college. I was newly married with an apartment to furnish and rent to pay. And I wrote for a living. I wrote whatever I could to make ends meet, some of it quite trivial in nature. As I approached thirty, and I began to get bored with simply typing out anything that anyone would pay me for, my work got far more intense, far more serious, and I wrote the series of books for which I'm famous. My whole reputation in science fiction is really based on the things I've done since the middle-1960s. I proceeded, then, to get far more elitist, more and more literary, to the point of no return, to the absolute vanishing point of my career. After my brief retirement, the book that I will return with will be far more accessible, far more human, far more concerned with matters of narrative rather than style. I don't see this so much as a selling-out of my former principles, but rather a logical outgrowth of my own self-examination in terms of my relationship *vis-a-vis* my readers. I think I wandered into very rarefied aesthetic realms, and now I've wandered back from there.

JE: Now that you're about to resume writing again, does the prospect excite you?

RS: Yes. However, I feel a certain apprehension after a four-year layoff. My new book, *Lord Valentine's Castle*, has already excited much comment and attention and, of course, a great deal of money. It's a major event, and I haven't done word one of it. So there's an element of uncertainty, which, I think, will go away once I actually sit down to write. I'm looking forward to starting. I would like to get the suspense over and find out what it feels like to write this book. But I don't plan to start for another few months. I want to tie up the loose ends in my life. I'm also hoping for another rainy winter to begin the book. I want it to nail me down indoors, without the temptation of going into the garden. All in all, it's a sense of anticipation, coupled with a bit of tension.

JE: Have you found that your image in the science fiction world has changed as a result of your retirement? Do science fiction readers view you differently today than they did previously?

RS: I think so. However, I haven't monitored that as closely as I might have. When I decided to quit, the reaction was two-fold: First, some people said, "Well, it's about time!" Second, others said, "He's so young, how can he break off his career just as he's reaching his stride? He owes us more books!" Both of these reactions eventually canceled each other out. The people who said, "It's about time," realized that that was a cruel and unjust attitude to take. And the people who said, "He owes us more books," began to perceive that I was very tired, that I needed a rest, and that I would come back when I was ready. Actually, that was something I didn't see myself. The fact that I had quit so publicly, almost unique in writing, and certainly in science fiction, focused a lot of retrospective attention on me. It was almost a posthumous feeling for me. People were summing up my career and, in the process, concluding that, yes, I did write a number of interesting books. I also got some perspective on my career during the layoff. I had written all those books, some fifteen in all, between 1966 and 1973. That's almost two books a year, which is an awful rush of stuff for people to digest in such a short period of time. I began to wonder, "Why haven't people noticed what I've done?" Well, they did notice, and there's a whole shelf of awards in my study to prove it. But it didn't seem to me as though the accomplishment had really sunk in. Well, after a few years in the garden to look at things more clearly, I realized that I simply asked too much of people; that they couldn't possibly absorb all of these books in so short a span of time. Now that they're being reissued gradually, people are picking them up and saying, "Far out, this guy has something. I want to read his other books." The effect has been one of a delayed impact. It was as though I had hurled all these skyrockets out and expected them to dazzle everybody all at once. All it did, though, was blind everyone. Now, people have had a chance to evaluate, to understand. When I told the publishers I was about to write another book, the response was very gratifying.

JE: Were you surprised by the enormous bid on your proposed new book,

Lord Valentine's Castle, by Harper & Row?

RS: Not really. I had been courted by publishers pretty steadily throughout the retirement period. What did surprise me, though, was that a hardcover publisher would make so large a bid. That's a tremendous vote of confidence. No hardcover publisher had ever risked that much on a science fiction book. Paperback people had paid nearly as much for books by writers less well known, so it was reasonable to assume that somebody would buy the book for $100,000 or $125,000. And I wasn't surprised by that. When Harper & Row reached out and said, "We have to have that book," it both pleased and amazed me.

JE: What explains this enormous show of commercial faith on their part?

RS: I think it's a sense on everybody's part that this is a break-through or break-out book. Everybody has known for a long time that I write well, that I write clean, comprehensible prose, that I tell an interesting story. As I've said, though, I permitted myself to move more and more in a private direction. As far as *Lord Valentine's Castle* is concerned, I've completed a substantive outline. It's not just a one-line proposal, but a detailed outline. And what that outline evidently said to the editors was, "Hey, he's finally going to get it together. He's going to give us that intensity of emotion and that cleanliness of prose. And he's going to tell a story that a million people will want to go out and read." So none of them wanted to be left out of the bidding on the chance that this book would be the one I've been building toward for twenty-five years. Simply put, they didn't want to lose their opportunity to buy into what they hope will be a big selling book.

JE: Did you feel any presure to return with a major book, a huge commercial success?

RS: No. I didn't feel pressure so much as I felt logic. I felt that if I came back at all, it shouldn't be with something piddling. I might just as well stay in my garden and play with my cacti as write a nothing kind of book. When I decided to resume writing again, it came quite out nowhere. I was out by the pool pruning a plant in the garden. Suddenly, there was a story idea in my head, which is not an amazing event for somebody who has written as many books as I have. But suddenly there was also something saying, "Write it!" I came into my office and jotted down a few lines about the book on the back of an envelope. It was just the barest sketch of what the book would be. I studied it for a moment, scratched my head, and said, "I really want to do this book." Then I asked myself the big question—namely, "Do I really want to get back into that jungle?" And the answer came back, "Yes." That evening I spoke to an editor, who happened to be in San Francisco at the time. I told him I wanted to write a book. And that man, who isn't going to publish it, put in a large bid, sight unseen, without knowing anything more about it. He said he would meet my minimal bid for the book. That gave me the courage, the willingness to go on and develop the full outline, which I ultimately sold to Harper & Row after an auction involving many publishers.

JE: To what extent did this book precipitate your return to writing, as opposed to merely being a convenient vehicle to accomplish the same objective?

RS: The book precipitated my decision. It will represent what I think of as a basic science fiction experience—that is, it will take the reader through strange places and show him wonders and marvels. That's what I always turned to science fiction for, beyond any other factor that it had to offer. In writing the book, it's important to me to experience these wonders and marvels simply to sustain my own interest in the project. The idea promised that. It was a trip I wanted to take. And I saw that if I did embark on that voyage, I would have a hell of a good time. Therefore, it's only logical to conclude that those who came along with me as readers would also have a good time. I could see immediately that this was a big book, a big audience, and big money which, of course, I'm not averse to. It was the right book to do—not simply one more in a series of books of the kind that I worked so hard on in the 1970s before I gave out. It's a book that's brand new, both in style and content.

JE: Can you say something, generally, about the proposed storyline of *Lord Valentine's Castle*?

RS: Well, at its simplest level, it's about a man of power who has lost his power—a disinherited prince—who embarks on an incredible odyssey of self-discovery, and eventually goes on to try to regain his lost power. It's basic prototypical fiction. Beyond that, I would rather not say much more about the story. I don't want everybody to feel that they've already read the book by the time I get around to writing it.

JE: Now that you've begun writing again, do you plan to return to regular production?

RS: I see my return as a one-shot effort. I'm no longer making great policy pronouncements about my career. When I made the retirement statement, it was for political effect and for cathartic value. I felt there were things wrong with the world of science fiction as of 1974, and I wanted to shake things up. Also, I needed to explain why I was getting out. I felt I couldn't just abandon my career without some kind of public accounting of the situation. Well, now I'm coming back with a book—*Lord Valentine's Castle*—and I don't know what I'll do after that. I'm taking one step at a time.

JE: As you resume writing today, how do you see your "new" audience?

RS: This book, I think, will appeal to a very broad segment of the science fiction audience. The range will include the reader who saw *Star Wars* a month ago and is just now finding his way into science fiction, to the reader who has been reading Roger Zelazny, Harlan Ellison, Michael Moorcock, and Robert Silverberg for the last fifteen years. Prior to this book, my readership consisted of a very narrow band of the science fiction audience. It was largely a college-educated, literary-oriented, sophisticated segment of the science fiction audience. These were people who were turned on by the imagery and the intellectual excitement of science fiction, but who also wanted the advanced stylistic amusement that typified my writing, as well as the emotional intensity and human interaction which are often lacking in science fiction. I want to keep those people as the nucleus of my audience, but I would hope to reach beyond them now. I want to go on serving their needs, but not their needs exclusively.

JE: Is that primarily a commercial decision on your part or does it reflect a genuine desire to reach different kinds of readers?

RS: Well, of course, it doesn't hurt commercially to have a larger audience but that isn't my basic goal. My main goal as a science fiction writer is to blow minds. That attitude underlies such books as *Son of Man, Tower of Glass,* and *Downward to the Earth.* In these books, I attempted to bombard the reader with emotions, images, and strangenesses. In my later books, the very dark, driven books, I limited the number of minds I could blow, simply by filtering out the reader who was simply looking for a good story. What I want to do now is reach as many people as possible with my kind of fiction. But these are not conscious, cynical, calculated decisions. I started this whole enterprise with a specific idea that came to me while I was minding my own business. I saw immediately that if I wrote this book, it would satisfy many of these requirements. It all fits together. Each part of this structure is intimately connected with everything else, and it all comes together at once. The publishers, looking at this idea, said, "Yeah, yeah, if he writes this book, we're all going to make a mint." And I'm all for that. This is a capitalist society. I find money very useful. I also have the hope, and this may be naive of me, but I don't think so, that the hundreds of thousands of people who read *Lord Valentine's Castle* will be turned on enough by that to go back and investigate *Dying Inside*, *Born with the Dead*, and *Son of Man*, books which did well, but did not grab a giant audience the first time around. They may see in those books the things I hope and think are in them.

JE: When you retired in 1974, you observed, "When I think of how my career in science fiction ended, I feel sad, bitter and confused." Do you still feel that way?

RS: No. In 1974, I felt that way, but I've now worked myself through a lot of those feelings. The statement that you referred to was partly a result of the fatigue that I mentioned, partly a result of circumstances in my private life, and partly my disappointment over the fact that I had thrown forth upon the world such books as *Nightwings*, *The Book of Skulls*, *Born with the Dead*, *Tower of Glass*, and all the others, only to discover that they had been woefully neglected, misunderstood, and unappreciated. That may sound like a terribly self-pitying kind of statement, but I felt a lot of self-pity in 1974. I've now had a long time to look at things, and I can see that, in fact, my career was quite enviable in 1974, and had I not been so tired, confused, and bitter, I would have realized I was in a much better position and simply needed a good rest.

JE: When you write science fiction these days, can you still say, as you once did, that you're a man who's living his adolescent fantasies, often through your writing?

RS: I've never lived my childhood or boyhood fantasies through science fiction. But I've certainly lived my boyhood or childhood fantasies, though. The reading of science fiction has been relatively unimportant to me for a long time. I do keep up with the outstanding books of the year, but I don't devour the stuff. When I said I was living my childhood or boyhood fantasies, it had to do with the fact that my youthful dreams and hopes have become a reality—namely, to be a highly successful and respected science fiction writer. Moreover, my success in this field has enabled me to live other fantasies having to do with sex, travel, money, and all the other wonderful things we dream of in childhood or adolescence. All in all, I've had a very satisfactory life, with several bumpy episodes in it. The bumps, thank God, have been well-spaced. And all of these experiences, both good and bad, are reflected in my writing, even though they may not have been concious decisions on my part.

JE: In what sense has science fiction's hold on you changed in recent years?

RS: Well, after I stopped writing it, I also stopped reading it, except as it related to my responsibilities as an editor. But I no longer felt in the center of things, in the feedback process. I didn't really care what was going on in the field because I didn't need to learn anything from it. I read science fiction when I had the time. But it was different. I didn't read it, as I once had, for professional purposes or psychic nourishment. In truth, though, the hold is still there. The fact, that when I came back, after all of this time, it was with a science fiction book, indicates that whatever virus I was inoculated with at the age of seven, eight, or nine is still raging somewhere through my system. I still buy all of the science fiction magazines, even though I barely read them. The idea of not buying *Fantasy & Science Fiction*, not buying *Analog*—these are things I've done since I was twelve years old. It's inconceivable not to do that, even though I know I'm not going to read them. Now, that's a deep-rooted infection.

JE: Given your skill at writing non-fiction, why did you decide to return with a science fiction book as opposed to a non-fiction work?

RS: I never considered returning as a non-fiction writer. I've written a good deal of non-fiction. It was very rewarding and interesting for the years I was doing it, but I grew awfully tired of writing it. I simply burned out on being an explainer of things to other people, which is what I was doing. And during my retirement, I felt, fundamentally, I was never going to write again. But if I ever did, I knew it would be with something that came from my emotional center; non-fiction rarely does. It certainly didn't for me. I wrote books that were intellectually interesting for me. If I wanted to know more about a subject, I would write a book about it. I don't feel that compulsion now. I'm terribly interested in certain areas of plants, for example, but I wouldn't write a book about them, even now, when I'm considering the notion of writing again. But certainly during the years when I was an ex-writer, there wasn't the slightest inclination to write more books of the non-fiction type.

JE: Do you think you've overcome the stereotype of a writer who's known for mass-produced, formularized stories?

RS: Well, certainly, I've overcome the formularized aspect because so much time has passed. Whole generations of science fiction readers have emerged who associate me with the very carefully crafted novels of the 1960s and 1970s rather than with the slap-dash stuff that I turned out in the 1950s. They just don't believe that the same man could have written both kinds of books and, in fact, the same man didn't, at least in the deepest sense of the word. But the mass-produced aspect still seems to linger. Some people have the feeling, since they know I wrote so prolifically, that I can still knock out a book in a week or two. They don't realize, because they weren't there while I was doing it, that the books of the last few years took me a long time to write. For example, *Shadrach in the Furnace* was a six-month project. *Born with the Dead*, which is only 20,000 words long, took me four months to complete. In 1957, I would have written a 20,000 word story in three days. It would not, however, have been *Born with the Dead*. I don't know how long *Lord Valentine's Castle* will take me to write. It's going to be a very big book. I hope to complete it in nine or ten months. I may find out, though, that it takes me much longer than that. Mass production—no! That's over with me forever.

JE: What accounts for the electrifying speed with which you were able to produce so many books during your most prolific years as a writer?

RS: I've thought about it many times. It's even difficult for me to understand how I was able to write so rapidly. But I do remember, though, how I did it. Essentially, it required total concentration. It was the sort of superhuman feat that might be equaled by a champion baseball player or weight lifter or discus thrower. I concentrated on a point source and the words just came out right, primarily because I was involved in a kind of self-hypnosis. That broke down, though. That kind of maniacal ability to concentrate, and the prolificness which accompanied it, however, are not things that I really mourn. I simply changed. It was, in every sense of the word, an athletic feat. I was last at the peak of it in the middle-1960s, when I was thirty-three or thirty-four years old, and wrote *Masks of Time*, took a breath and wrote *Son of Man*, and took a breath and wrote *Man in the Maze*. Now, I look back at that period and wonder how I ever did it. That kind of thing will never happen again.

JE: When you think about what you're capable of producing and what you've actually produced, how do you assess where you're at at this particular moment in time? Do you feel good about what you've been able to do, when measured against what you're capable of doing?

RS: If I had to do it all over again, it would probably come out pretty much the same way. The early years were years of apprenticeship, learning the discipline, mastering the formulas. The formulas are important now. These were years of learning that dreadful facility. And even though I wrote some awful garbage during that period, I think it all went into creating the writer who eventually emerged. Then there were the years of giving back all that I had learned. I'm very pleased with the books I wrote then. I wrote the kind of science fiction I wanted to read. More than that I couldn't ask of myself. I rarely read my own books, but when I do, it's with pleasure. Then I hit the dead-end, the moment of silence, the long period of self-examination, and that was necessary, too. And now I'm about to add the one thing that was missing from the whole pattern, which was the big strong narrative novel. There's nothing like that in my ten-mile shelf of books. So I will put in the missing piece. I see it as a very coherent pattern, heading straight toward *Lord Valentine's Castle*, although I didn't know that until a month ago.

JE: As you review the multitude of books which bear your name, are you able to discern clear signs of growth, maturation, stylistic improvement?

RS: Yes, very much so. In 1958, I wrote a book entitled, *Recalled to Life*. I thought it was a masterpiece when I wrote it. To me, it was clearly a first-rate novel. You need that kind of confidence to produce any kind of writing, especially, if you're going to be as prolific as I was. In this case, I felt the book really stood out. Well, it was published, but it didn't win a Hugo award. Many people, however, dropped me post cards and said, "Yes, that's a pretty good book." In 1970, a new edition of that book came out. I reread it to see how good that masterpiece was. I discovered it was pretty awful. Only twelve years had passed, but I could see the clumsiness of style, the downright foolishness of plot. Now, I thought I knew it all when I was twenty-two. When I looked at that book again, at the age of thirty-five, I realized I hadn't known it all. Now, when I look back at the books I wrote when I was thirty-five, I also see, occasionally, a grammatical error, a flossy sentence, an unclear reference. And so, on the level of craft, of carpentry, of hammer and nails, there's been a steady growth that simply emerges from working with the materials and learning how to use the tools better. Then, of course, there's the fact that at forty-three, you know much more about yourself and other human beings than you did at twenty-two, because you've had a long time to look. And unless you're totally without perception, in which case you shouldn't be a writer, you observe things and you learn them. Things happen to you as you get older, which make you a better writer. At the time I wrote *Thorns*, for example, I had never been to Australia. I had never had the experience of watching my house burn down. I had never been through a marital break-up. I could sit here for hours just listing those things that happened to me in the thirteen years since I wrote *Thorns*. Because those things hadn't happened then, that book is a less complex expression of a human being than the books I wrote after that. And I can see the scars and blood stains of my autobiography all over the books that I wrote, even though none of them, including *Dying Inside*, are specifically autobiographical. But all of them are, generally, autobiographical. It's impossible to avoid that.

JE: I'm sure you knew then, and do now, that you could still sell books without aspiring to a higher and higher level of craftsmanship. If that's true, what accounts for your desire to write better and better books? Does the market impose that standard on you?

RS: Actually, the market attempted to force me in the opposite direction. Part of it, I suppose, is pride. I'm not immune to pride. Part of it, also, is my low tolerance of boredom. After turning out inferior copy for many years, I needed some motivation other than making another dollar to go on writing. I have to retain my own interest, to continually challenge and stimulate myself. Moreover, part of it is a highly moral, terribly conscientious-sounding thing—that is, when I was a boy, I read science fiction and it did wonderful things for me. It opened the universe to me. I feel a sense of obligation to science fiction to replace what I had taken from it, to add to the shelf, to put something there for someone else that would do for them what other writers had done for me. Now, when I began as a science fiction writer, turning out all those mass-produced, formularized books, I certainly wasn't serving science fiction. I was serving my landlord and my other creditors. So there was a strong compulsion to atone for those early dollar-earners. I wanted to leave behind books such as *Downward to the Earth, Tower of Glass, Son of Man, The Book of Skulls*, and be able to say to the reader, "Hey, I made these for you the same way that H. G. Wells made *The Time Machine* for me."

JE: As you begin to write again, do you perceive any new directions that your work might take?

RS: Well, of course, I'm not beginning to write again. What I'm doing is writing *Lord Valentine's Castle*, making no commitments beyond that. I'll find out when I begin writing. I believe the book will come easily to me, certainly more easily than the last few books did. Those last few books were written against terrible inner resistance. The planning of *Lord Valentine's Castle*, though, came with great ease. And that is reassuring to me. From the original one-line story idea to the eighteen-page outline which followed, the entire effort was done without hindrance. An interesting thing happened in the course of planning the book, which reminds me of one of the great joys of writing. I had written a complete draft of the outline and thought it was quite satisfactory. As I was retyping the outline to send to my agent, I came to the final sentence of the book and discovered that something was wrong. Indeed, a major plot transformation occurred right at the typewriter while I was doing a simple typing job. It's that sense of surprise, of discovery, that makes writing so delightful.

JE: Were there moments during your retirement when, in the wee hours of the morning, you returned to the typewriter and attempted to write a short story or something else? Did you ever feel the urge to write?

RS: I never actually worked in the wee hours of the morning. But I did occasionally dream that I was writing again. Whenever that happened, which occured once or twice, I would wake up in a cold sweat. I did make one reluctant effort to write again during the retirement period, not voluntarily, but only as a favor to a very close friend. After he pressed me for over a year, I finally relented and decided to give it a try. However, I tried and failed. I couldn't motivate myself to do the work. But that was a project coming from outside myself, and, obviously, I was resisting it even while I was attempting to do it. When *Lord Valentine's Castle* came, it came completely spontaneously from within. Only a few days before, I had turned down a $50,000 writing project. Again, it was someone who had an idea and wanted me to do it. I said, "No, that's a lovely pile of money, but I'll never be able to bring myself to do it." And suddenly came this magical idea a few days later, at which point I said to myself, "I'll do it!" I've never been good at responding to authority. That's one of the occupational hazards, I guess, of an entire lifetime spent as a freelance writer. I can't do what other people tell me to.

JE: Admittedly, you're a serious writer of fiction, one who aspires to certain artistic standards. Does science fiction accommodate those concerns? Have you outgrown the genre?

RS: Well, I certainly thought that during my retirement. I had tried in those increasingly difficult and sophisticated books of the early 1970s to expand the artistic possibilities of science fiction. And I had my head handed to me for trying it, or so it seemed. That greatly disillusioned me. I feel a lot mellower about the whole thing now. I think that science fiction still has certain fundamental limits having to do with the fact that it deals with the real world at one or two metaphorical levels removed, but that it's also a hell of a wonderful vehicle for the imagination. If I've grown weary of it as a reader, it's because I've read nineteen miles of it and need a vacation from it for awhile. If I grew weary of it as a writer, it was for the same reasons. I would still, I think, place Joyce's *Ulysses* higher than *Stranger in a Strange Land*, but it would be a pity to be without Heinlein's works just as it would be a pity if we were denied Joyce's talents. I would be the poorer to lose either.

JE: What about the science fiction genre interests and excites you today?

RS: Basically, the same things that excited me when I was nine years old. It shows me things I couldn't see otherwise. I don't go to science fiction for social satire. I don't go to science fiction for criticism of society. I can do that by just looking at the newspaper and muttering to myself. I go to science fiction for sweep, for vision, for beauty, for the mother ship hanging overhead, for those special moments of wonder. Admittedly, it's harder and harder to find them. It's much easier to have your mind blown when you're twelve years old. But I can still find them occasionally, and it's in that hope that I keep going back. And I still find them, much to my amazement and pleasure.

JE: Clearly, you're known as a superstar in the science fiction world. What explains your failure to find critical acceptance and attention in the broader literary world?

RS: There's an ugly paradox involved here. The people who read mainstream novels know they don't like science fiction. The same thing is true in the field of mystery novels. A writer like Ross Macdonald, who was writing first-rate novels that happen to be about a detective, spent years being submerged as a mystery writer. For example, I don't like detective novels, and so it would never have occurred to me to read a Ross Macdonald novel. I just don't like that kind of book. Western writers are faced with the same thing. People who read John

Updike and John Cheever don't read westerns. And people who read Updike and Cheever know they don't like science fiction, unless they pick it up out of curiosity or accident, hearing that a particular book has received a great deal of attention. They might pick up a science fiction book, but if it's the wrong one, then they'll never come back. Well, that attitude did a lot of harm to me. I ended up falling into a very deep chasm, because the Updike and Cheever audience didn't read me, since I was a science fiction writer, and the science fiction audience didn't read me, since they felt I was too much like Updike and Cheever. For a little while in the 1970s, nobody was reading me. Well, I've survived that very nicely, thank you, but it was a rough period for me.

JE: Finally, what hopes do you have for *Lord Valentine's Castle* in terms of impact? What would you like your readers to come away with after reading the book?

RS: I'm very concerned with impact. And I think my books do have impact. In the end, I want to leave my readers a little dazed, blinking a bit as the sparkles fade from their eyes, changed. I don't want this book to serve as a time-passer, but I want it to pass through their consciousness and leave them forever seeing the universe in a different way. I hope I've accomplished that in some of my books and will do so again in *Lord Valentine's Castle*.

THE MILFORD SERIES: Popular Writers of Today

1. *Robert A. Heinlein: Stranger in His Own Land,* by George Edgar Slusser
2. *Alistair MacLean: The Key is Fear*, by Robert A. Lee
3. *The Farthest Shores of Ursula K. LeGuin*, by George Edgar Slusser
4. *The Bradbury Chronicles*, by George Edgar Slusser
5. *John D. MacDonald and the Colorful World of Travis McGee*, by Campbell
6. *Harlan Ellison: Unrepentant Harlequin*, by George Edgar Slusser
7. *Kurt Vonnegut: The Gospel from Outer Space*, by Clark Mayo
8. *The Space Odysseys of Arthur C. Clarke*, by George Edgar Slusser
9. *Aldiss Unbound: The Science Fiction of Brian Aldiss*, by Richard Mathews
10. *The Delany Intersection: Samuel R. Delany*, by George Edgar Slusser
11. *The Classic Years of Robert A. Heinlein*, by George Edgar Slusser
12. *The Dream Quest of H. P. Lovecraft*, by Darrell Schweitzer
13. *Worlds Beyond the World: William Morris*, by Richard Mathews
15. *Lightning from a Clear Sky: J. R. R. Tolkien*, by Richard Mathews
17. *Conan's World and Robert E. Howard*, by Darrell Schweitzer
18. *Against Time's Arrow: Poul Anderson*, by Sandra Miesel
19. *The Clockwork Universe of Anthony Burgess*, by Richard Mathews
20. *The Haunted Man: The Strange Genius of David Lindsay*, by Colin Wilson
21. *Colin Wilson: The Outsider and Beyond*, by Clifford P. Bendau
22. *A Poetry of Force and Darkness: John Hawkes*, by Eliot Berry
23. *Science Fiction Voices #1*, edited by Darrell Schweitzer
24. *A Clash of Symbols: James Blish*, by Brian M. Stableford
25. *Science Fiction Voices #2*, edited by Jeffrey M. Elliot
26. *Earth Is The Alien Planet: J. G. Ballard*, by David Pringle

Ready late 1979: 14. *Frank Herbert: Prophet of Dune*, by George Edgar Slusser
Ready Apr. 1980: 16. *I. Asimov*, by George Edgar Slusser
Ready Apr. 1980: 27. *Literary Voices #1*, edited by Jeffrey M. Elliot
Ready Apr. 1980: 28. *The Rainbow Quest of Thomas Pynchon*, by D. A. Mackey
Ready Apr. 1980: 29. *Science Fiction Voices #3*, edited by Jeffrey M. Elliot
Ready Apr. 1980: 30. *Still Worlds Collide: Philip Wylie*, by Clifford P. Bendau

All books $2.95 (Paper) and $8.95 ((Cloth). To order, please send price plus $1.00 for postage and handling to The Borgo Press, Box 2845, San Bernardino, CA 92406, USA. California residents must add 6% sales tax.

Introducing

a new magazine for the discriminating SF reader who had trouble keeping track of the 1,000+ titles of science fiction and fantasy published during 1978

☞ Send us a 15¢ stamp and find out why

Science Fiction & Fantasy Book Review

A BORGO PRESS PUBLICATION

will save you time and money

- Issued monthly for up-to-date reviews of all new books while still available.
- Comprehensive coverage of American science fiction, fantasy, weird supernatural fiction, nonfiction books about SF, calendars, art books, small press items.
- Selective coverage of British and foreign language first editions.
- Edited by Neil Barron, Author of ANATOMY OF WONDER, the best annotated bibliography of science fiction.
- Published by R. Reginald, Author of SCIENCE FICTION AND FANTASY LITER—ATURE, the standard bibliography of fantastic literature.
- Science fiction and fantasy awards and their winners.
- Obituaries of leading figures and writers in the field.
- Special reports on SF publishing, both here and abroad.
- Review articles on selected writers and movements.
- Retrospective reviews of little-known books that deserve a better fate.
- All issues mailed at first class rates (so you get them next week, and not next month)

Write now for your **FREE** sample copy of issue #1.

☞ **SCIENCE FICTION & FANTASY BOOK REVIEW**
P.O. Box 2845, San Bernardino, California 92406

(or send us $12 for a charter subscription)